The Good Book Big Book Guidebook

Dick B.'s Reference Titles on Alcoholics Anonymous History
Paradise Research Publications, Inc., Publisher;
Good Book Publishing Company, Distributor P.O. Box 837, Kihei, HI 96753-0837
Phone/Fax: (808) 874 4876; Email: dickb@dickb.com; URL: http://www.dickb.com/index.shtml

Publisher's December 1, 2005 List of Titles by Author Dick B.; All list prices: Effective December 1, 2005

Anne Smith's Journal, 1933-1939, 3rd ed.; 1998; 6 x 9; 180 pp.; $16.95

By the Power of God: A Guide to Early A.A. Groups & Forming Similar Groups Today; 2000, 6 x 9; 260 pp., $16.95

Cured!: Proven Help for Alcoholics and Addicts; 2003, 6 x 9; 182 pp., $17.95

Dr. Bob and His Library, 3rd ed.; 1998; 6 x 9; 156 pp.; $15.95

God and Alcoholism: Our Growing Opportunity in the 21st Century; 2002; 6 x 9; 190 pp.; $17.95

Good Morning!: Quiet Time, Morning Watch, Meditation, and Early A.A.; 2d ed.; 1998; 6 x 9; 154 pp.; $16.95

Henrietta B. Seiberling: Ohio's Lady with a Cause, Rev. ed.; 2004; 46 pp.; 6 x 9; $15.95

Making Known The Biblical History and Roots of Alcoholics Anonymous: An Eleven-Year Research, Writing, Publishing and Fact Dissemination Project, 2001, 160 pp., spiral bound, $24.95

New Light on Alcoholism: God, Sam Shoemaker, and A.A.; 2d ed.; 1999; 6 x 9; 672 pp.; $24.95

The Akron Genesis of Alcoholics Anonymous, 2d ed.; 1998; 6 x 9; 400 pp.; $17.95

The Books Early AAs Read for Spiritual Growth, 7th ed.; 1998; 6 x 9; 126 pp.; $15.95

The First Nationwide A.A. History Conference - Comments of Dick B., 2003, 6 x 9; $17.95

The Golden Text of A.A.: God, the Pioneers, and Real Spirituality; 1999; 6 x 9; 76 pp.; $14.95

The Good Book and The Big Book: A.A.'s Roots in the Bible; 2d ed.; 1997; 6 x 9; 264 pp.; $17.95

The James Club: The Original A.A. Program's Absolute Essentials, 3rd ed., 2005; 6 x 9; $17.95

The Oxford Group & Alcoholics Anonymous, 2d ed.; 1998; 6 x 9; 432 pp.; $17.95

That Amazing Grace (Clarence & Grace S.); 1996; 6 x 9; 160 pp.; $16.95

Turning Point: A History of Early A.A.'s Spiritual Roots and Successes; 1997; 6 x 9; 776 pp.; $29.95

Twelve Steps for You: Let Our Creator, A.A. History, and the Big Book Be Your Guide; 2003; 6 x 9; 90 pp. $17.95

Utilizing Early A.A.'s Spiritual Roots for Recovery Today; Rev. ed.; 1999; 6 x 9; 106 pp., $14.95

When Early AA s Were Cured and Why; 2003; 6 x 9; $17.95

Why Early A.A. Succeeded: The Good Book in Alcoholics Anonymous Yesterday and Today (a Bible Study Primer), 2001; 6 x 9; 340 pp., $17.95

Available through other distributors

Hope: The Story of Geraldine O. Delaney, 2d ed. NJ: Alina Lodge

Our Faith Community A.A. Legacy (Dick B., ed and compiler). FL: Came to Believe Publications

Courage to Change (with Bill Pittman). MN: Hazelden

Women Pioneers of AA (Dick B., contributor). MN: Hazelden

The Good Book-Big Book Guidebook

How to Include the Creator's Impact on Early A.A. in Recovery Programs Today

Dick B.

Paradise Research Publications, Inc.
Kihei, Maui, Hawaii

Paradise Research Publications, Inc.
P.O. Box 837
Kihei, HI 96753-0837
URL: http://www.dickb.com/index.shtml
Email: dickb@dickb.com

© 2006 by Anonymous
All rights reserved.
Printed in the United States of America

Cover Design: Terry Dunford (American Creations of Maui)

This Paradise Research Publications Edition is published by arrangement with Good Book Publishing Company, PO Box 837, Kihei, HI 96753-0837

The publication of this volume does not imply affiliation nor approval nor endorsement from Alcoholics Anonymous World Services, Inc.

ISBN: 1-885803-91-5

Contents

1. History: The Inclusion in Recovery of A.A.'s Biblical Origins and Christian Fellowship 1

    Some Questions for You 1
    Suggestions for Your Approach 4
    "The Twenty Questions 10

2. The Healing Evidence at the Time When A.A. Was Born 21

    Miracles Never Ceased 21
    Recognition of the Efficacy of Healings 22

3. Alcoholics Anonymous, the Founders, Belief in Almighty God and Divine Healing 31

    Without Any Apparent Exception, A.A.'s Founders Believed the Creator Cured Them 31
    The Dramatic Denial in Later A.A. 33
    Let's Look at the Bible Early AAs Were Studying for Basic Ideas about Healing and Cure 36
    Let's Look at the Believers Who Healed Throughout History 39

4. The Spiritual Beginnings of A.A. 55

    A.A.: Unique, But Borrowed 55
    Two Distinctly Different Spiritual Origins 56
    The New York Genesis and its Dr. Carl Jung/Rev. Sam Shoemaker Source 56
    The Akron Genesis and its Bible/Dr. Bob Source 58
    The Christian Endeavor Society Impact 60
    Melding the Roots was solely a Bill Wilson Project 63

5. The Real Program of Early A.A. 65

    An Overview of What They Did in Akron 65

      The Frank Amos Reports in 1938 67
      The Major Biblical Roots of the Original Program ... 68

6. **The Materials from the Bible That Dr. Bob Considered "Absolutely Essential"** 73

      Introductory Comments 73
      The Bible Was King in the Early Program. You met and used it at every turn. 73
      The Picture of the Bible's Use 74
      Many of the Bible's Books, Parts, and Verses Need Specific Mention Here. 76
      Verses That Received Special Attention and Use 77
      The Special Role of the Books of Matthew, James, and 1 Corinthians 80
      The Book of James 96
      1 Corinthians 13 112

7. **The Approach Early Akron A.A.'s Took While They Sought Christian Healing** 117

      Identifying Their Alcoholism 117
      Popularity of the Disease Concept 117
      The Sin Concept 119
      Overcoming 122
      The Pioneer Approach 123

8. **The Practical Use and Application of This Guide** 125

      Where to Begin 125
      The Objective 131
      Your Particular Program 141
      Go and Tell 143

9. **Selected Bibliography** 145

10. **Appendix One** 155

      Catch the Wave 155

**The First Step: What Does our Heavenly Father say?
.... 156
The Second Step: To Be a Doer of the Word 159
The Third Step: Praise, Be Thankful, and Enjoy 160
Keep Your Love Light Shining..................................... 161
Put Your Heavenly Father First.................................... 161
Take Care of Yourself 161
Eliminate the Stress 161
See the Doctor Regularly... 162**

11. Appendix Two 163

**A.A. History Study Meetings 163
Studying the History, Bible Roots, Big Book, and
    Twelve Steps 163
Parts of the Good Book A.A. Old-Timers Considered
    "Absolutely Essential".. 164
Why this Guide is Needed 164
Begin with the Bible Itself... 166
James..167
Jesus' Sermon on the Mount 175
The Thirteenth Chapter of 1 Corinthians 177
Suggested Reading to Enrich Your Meetings and
    Individual Studies 179**

ix

1

History: The Inclusion in Recovery of A.A.'s Biblical Origins and Christian Fellowship

There are many recovery programs today. Some achieve fine results. But any and all could profit by adding a chapter, a segment, a chunk of history to their approaches—the history of the early A.A. Christian Fellowship program in Akron, its Bible roots, and its astonishing success..

Why? Because so much of the early A.A. 75% to 93% success rate among real medically incurable alcoholics hinged on the truths the pioneers studied and applied from the Holy Bible. The Bible they called the Good Book. In those great days, they didn't omit the Creator, His son Jesus Christ, the gift of the Holy Spirit, or the Bible. They counted on them.

And this is a Guidebook that suggests how you can incorporate that history in just about any recovery approach you use—in A.A. itself, other 12 Step fellowships, A.A. Big Book/Bible Study Groups, Christian Recovery Groups, Christ-centered recovery groups, Conventional treatment models, Christian Track Treatment Programs, Therapeutic Community and Rehab programs, para-church recovery groups, and a church's recovery outreach.

Take your pick. All could use some substantial beefing up when it comes to learning, absorbing, teaching, and applying the early A.A. Christian fellowship ideas. They were the basis for A.A.'s remarkable successes in the 1930's!

Some Questions for You

Questions: Let's start with some questions—for AAs and 12 Step members who are Christians; for Christian recovery groups within and outside A.A.; for Christian treatment programs; for treatment center leaders who are more and more including Christian Track in their offerings; for those who simply want to know more about A.A. and the Bible, or more about the basic ideas A.A. pioneers took from their study of the Bible, or more about A.A. and 12 Step links to Christianity. Also for those who are wondering if the history of early A.A. belongs as a part of their agenda:

- **Did you know that early A.A. in Akron was a Christian Fellowship?**

- **Did you know that its basic ideas came from AAs' study of the Bible?**

- **Did you know that their original Akron meetings were called "old fashioned prayer meetings?"**

- **Did you know that many of Akron's pioneer principles and practices derived from the United Christian Endeavor Society—a huge international young people's movement?**

- **Did you know that the Book of James, the Sermon on the Mount, and 1 Corinthians 13 were considered "absolutely essential" to their program?**

- **Did you know that the pioneers achieved a documented 75% to 93% success rate as the result of what they did in their program—and that these successes were widely and properly called "cures."**

- **Do you agree that a knowledge of these facts would strengthen and buttress any Christian Track, Christian Recovery, Christian 12-Step, or Christ-centered Recovery Program?**

- **If you wanted to overcome alcoholism or teach about and treat how to cure of alcoholism, wouldn't you want to know as much as possible about exactly how the early AAs did that?**

- **Do you realize that most people who are sent to 12 Step programs by the courts or by treatment centers or by therapists just aren't sent there with any thoughts or expectations as to God, Jesus Christ, the Bible, Christian healing, or Christian A.A. history?**

- **The challenge for you today—Where to find the facts, and how to present them**: People who are entrusted with recovery work, whether as A.A. sponsors or in some other capacity, usually haven't a clue about the foregoing matters. But where would you go for the facts? What are the reliable sources? Who shall, and how shall you, present the materials? In what way can a segment be incorporated in existing programs? Certainly not without your knowing the history.

For decades, historians, professionals, and AAs themselves have drifted away from the early history and drifted toward idolatrous "deities" like a higher power, a lightbulb, a radiator, "Something,," and often an undefined "spirituality" that requires no belief at all. This drift certainly opened wide the doors to secularization of groups, to hordes of non-religious treatment centers hungry for clients, for enormous "spiritual but no religious" book sales, and for substitute "model" programs.

In addition, however, it often left most newcomers with the belief that early A.A. really didn't work that well, that most of the pioneers got drunk, that the present-day relapses are OK, to be expected, understandable, "treatable," and will be overcome with "spirituality" (but never religion). Mostly, the new "spirituality" is more about "no god" or "not-god" than it is about establishing a relationship with the one, true, living God. There is simply little talk in A.A. today, or in writings about 12 Step programs, that tells people how much early AAs originally learned and believed about the Creator's healing power and impact on Alcoholics Anonymous or about the Bible's role and importance.

History—accurate, concisely presented, illuminating history—can help. It can provide a new foundation for successful teaching. Of course, it's not the history itself that is vital. It's the power of the

Creator. And it's about learning His key role in 1935—the year A.A. was founded.

Suggestions for Your Approach

Devoting a segment to what A.A. pioneers really did. We'll not presume to say that all approaches to filling the history gap are or should be identical. We do believe and urge that a portion of any recovery approach should be devoted to history. Incidentally, many of the early A.A. ideas that were taken from the Bible rest, in turn, on the many writings of the Rev. Samuel Moor Shoemaker, Jr., a "Bible Christian" and Rector of Calvary Church in New York, whose books were widely read by Akron AAs (See Dick B., *New Light on Alcoholism: God, Sam Shoemaker, and A.A.*, 2nd ed., Paradise Research Publications, Inc., 1999)

To be sure, A.A. and other 12-Step programs already have their materials in place. Treatment programs and therapists are already steeped in method. Christian programs, whether totally Christian or a Christian-track presentation, may already cover Christian ideas and Bible verses. But all need an historical supplement to their approach to people in need—a segment that gives the facts about the Christian program of the 1930's that was already in place and very successful.

Most existing programs already have a curriculum. Thus Alcoholics Victorious and Overcomers Outreach, Inc. already have a full plate. Even so, both regularly order and presumably offer Dick B. titles already. But we suggest the following resources they could possibly use to add a historical segment or series to their curricula. So too many of the Christian Track treatment programs. So too most Twelve Step programs, including A.A.

For, in most all of these cases, there is gross inadequacy when it comes to practical history resources now in use. The suggestions here can certainly also apply to newcomers, sponsors, meetings, groups, Big Book/Bible study groups, Step-study groups, seminars, panels, conferences, and resource agencies.

Whatever their program or agenda, all could stand a solid, beefed up information approach and resource. An approach and additional resource that need not dilute programs in place. But an approach that tells it like it was, instead of like it is.

Furthermore, if anyone wants to apply these suggestions as well to an "Old School A.A." approach in the context of his own program and approach, this Guidebook and its suggestions will fit the bill. Details on resources to acquire and use are included in the concluding chapter of the Guide.

The following—detailed by other, later materials in this guidebook-- outline historical items that ought to be added or may be added to the thousands of existing programs and groups today. Every one of the items is historical in character. Every one was involved in the early A.A. program in one way or another. And every one could bless the newcomer today and enrich any program in which he is enrolled.

The reader can determine which, or which part, or whether all, will fit in the appropriate slot of his program. If nothing more, the material can be used to bring history out of the darkness by describing the approaches of the early Christian Fellowship of alcoholics in Akron.

Elements that can profitably be included, in whole or in part:

1. Adopting an historical framework as to outreach:

Contact with the newcomer: At meetings, by referral, by interview, by admission, by intervention, by phone and email inquiries, by intervention, and by "Twelfth Steppers." The pioneers reached the new people in many of these ways; and 12 Step workers still do.

Arranging medical help: The first stop is the hospital, the detox unit, or at least a doctor. That was a "must" in early A.A.; and it should be a "must" today. I've been to too many meetings, including one of my own first meetings, where a newcomer is red-faced, sweating, shaking, and confused—on the brink, in some cases like my own, of having seizures. I was ignored, until I actually had the grand-mal seizures and almost bit off my tongue whereas I had previously been told to take "orange juice and honey." But fooling with a newcomer like that without dealing with medical problems, acute withdrawal, "D,T,'s," and seizures and without regard for his initial medical problems is just plain dangerous. He may have alcohol-related illness, injuries, and potential acute withdrawal potential. Early AAs took no chances. They hospitalized the newcomer in almost every case. And, as a sidelight, it gave them a real opportunity to tell him their stories, introduce him to surrender, and have him accept Christ.

Paralleling the first live-in, free "halfway houses." As often as not, a newcomer was brought to the home of Anne and Dr. Bob, or Wally G. and his wife, Tom Lucas and his wife, and Clarence Snyder and his wife. At personal expense, these wonderful old-timers provided free housing, free meals, and a free long-term opportunity for "resident" counseling and indoctrination. Temptation was substantially eliminated. The results showed!

Utilizing a weekly Biblically oriented meeting coupled withmore frequent in-house fellowship meetings. The pioneers had no Big Book. They had no Steps.They had no drunk-a-logs. When they met, they heard the Bible read; they prayed; they sought guidance; and they received Christian devotionals and literature to read. Meetings were not required, but they did provide a source of protection, indoctrination, and unity. Dr. Bob called every meeting a Christian Fellowship.

2. Defining alcoholism for the newcomer:

(a) A Disease? Not a great deal was known about alcoholism or the technique for cure thereof in 1935. In fact the malady was considered "medically" incurable. Obeisance was paid to the "disease" idea of an allergy, an obsession, and a progressive illness. But that approach left programs with such words as "powerless," "incurable," and "only a daily reprieve. And that information was passed along to us today..

There are wide variety of views as to what constitutes alcoholism. See Dick B., *God and Alcoholism*. The so-called father of the "disease concept" was E.W. Jellinek, and his foundational book was *The Disease Concept of Alcoholism*. New Brunswick, NJ: Hillhouse Press, 1960. Yet it was Jellinek himself who cautioned:

"... one must conclude that there are more definitions of definition than there are 'definitions' of alcoholism" (p. 33).

(b) *Reviewing actual experiences themselves:* I have used the various tests below and they are very helpful. Yet I have concluded that, for the purpose of working with a newcomer as I do, it's better to talk about what I know. And what I know is that my alcoholism (and that of most in the A.A. fellowship) can be described with three "D's" and an "R."—Drink, Drunk, Disaster, and Return. That pretty much sums up our plight: We Drink too much. We get Drunk too often; and we probably look forward to getting drunk again. We encounter Disaster time after time—whether accidents, fights, legal problems, financial problems, family problems, jail, arrests, hangovers, ill-health, the shakes, the blackouts, and all the rest. And yet we Return, again and again, to repeat the cycle.

It takes no time at all for one alcoholic to compare notes with another and at least define alcoholic experiences galore. We speak a basic language whether our experience involved booze, bongs, or ice.

(c) *Sin?* There's also the problem of "sin." It's discussed about as well and thoroughly by a distinguished theology professor and prolific writer who is frequently quoted and only recently passed away. He is The Reverend Howard Clinebell, Ph.D., Emeritus Professor of Theology, Claremont, California. Clinebell spent many decades researching alcoholism, A.A., A.A. history, and pastoral counseling of alcoholics and addicts. One of his last works was *Understanding and Counseling Persons with Alcohol, Drug, and Behavioral Additions.* Nashville: Abingdon, 1998.

At pages 287-299, Clinebell discusses a wide variety of views on whether or not alcoholism is sin or is a sin. His views should be examined in company with those of the lay Baptist preacher and recovered alcoholic Jerry G. Dunn who wrote the widely sold. *God is for the Alcoholic.* Chicago, Moody Press, 1965. It would be useful also to familiarize yourself with the unceasing batterings on this topic by the Psychoheresy group, headed by the two Bobgans.

Altogether these views make it quite clear that there are diversities of views of sin, sinful conduct, and sins. All of which cause Christians to differ, writers and religious to spurn the "disease" concept and 12 Step programs, and certain denominations to reject any but religious approaches designed to deal with the sin problem.

I won't join the fray, but I will cite some Bible materials that are, and ought to be taken into consideration if you are dealing with Christians who love the Word of God.

Ephesians 5:18:

> And be not drunk with wine, wherein is excess; but be filled with the Spirit.

Galatians 5:16, 19-21:

> This I say then, Walk in the Spirit, and ye shall not fulfil the lust of the flesh. . . . Now the works of the flesh are manifest, which are these: Adultery, fornication, uncleanness, 1 asciviousness, Idolatry, withcraft, hatred, variance, emulations, wrath, strife, seditions, heresies. Envyings, murders, drunkenness, revellings and such like. . .

Romans 13:12-14:

> The night is far spent, the day is at hand: let us therefore cast off the works of darkness, and put on the amour of light. Let us walk honestly, as in the days, not in rioting and drunkenness, and in chambering and wantonness, not in strife and envying. But put ye on the Lord Jesus Christ, and make not provision for the flesh, to fulfil the lusts thereof.

Romans 14:21:

> It is good neither to eat flesh, nor to drink wine, nor any thing whereby thy brother stumbleth, or is offended, or is made weak.

1 Thessalonians 5:21-22:

> Prove all things; hold fast that which is good. Abstain from all appearance of evil.

1 Timothy 3:1-2, 8:

> A bishop then must be blameless, the husband of one wife, vigilant, sober, of good behavior, given to hospitality, apt to teach; Not given to wine, no striker, not greedy of filthy lucre; but patient, not a brawler, not covetous. . . . Likewise must the deacons be grave, not double tongued, not given to much wine, not greedy of filthy lucre.

Then there is the classic recital in Proverbs 23:29-35 which begins:

> "Who hath woe? Who hath sorrow? Who hath contentions? Who hath babbling, who hath wounds without cause? Who hath redness of eyes? They that tarry long at the wine; they that go to seek mixed wine."

The chapter concludes with this:

> "They have stricken me, shalt thou say, and I was not sick; they have beaten me, and I felt it not: when shall I awake? I will seek it yet again."

Drink. Drunk. Disaster. Return. To be sure, there are Bible students and scholars who argue "wine" doesn't mean "real wine." There are also those claim the Bible does not forbid drinking (which it doesn't), and those who disagree. There are those who believe that all the foregoing verses add up to God's command that we are not to be drunken or drink to excess. If so, excessive drinking and drunkenness are surely sins, from the Biblical standpoint.

Suppose they are. Is there any reason at all that this point should not be covered today? It certainly was in early A.A.—even in some of the earlier language of the Twelve Steps and in the descriptions of the

Akron program. Who should be afraid to say "sin"—especially when speaking in an historical or Biblical context?

3. Gaining the alcoholic's admission of his alcoholism: In early A.A., the alcoholic was to identify and admit his problem. As to how he did this before the Big Book was published, I can only speculate. But it seems likely that the following tests may have been submitted to him or their contents may have been related to him, whether in articulated form or by conversation. I have found them useful in helping newcomers "to fully concede to our innermost selves that we were alcoholics" (*Alcoholics Anonymous*, 4th ed., p. 30)concede to his innermost self that he is alcoholic They suggest to the inquiring alcoholic:

> *A "real alcoholic" is:* Someone who has lost the ability to control his drinking (See *Alcoholics Anonymous*, 4th ed., p. 30).
>
> ***Two basic tests***: If, when you start drinking, you lose control over the amount you take; or if, when you honestly want to quit, you can't quit entirely, you are "probably" an alcoholic (See *Alcoholics Anonymous*, 4th ed., p. 44).
>
> ***The old "Twenty Questions"*** tendered in various forms:

(These have been phrased in different manners, and sometimes the questions were different. But one typical test would say: If you answered "yes" to one, you probably are an alcoholic; and if you answered "yes" to three, you are definitely an alcoholic. See:

"The Twenty Questions

Does drinking cause you problems?

These questions relate to common problems with using alcohol. Only you can decide if you have a "drinking problem" and whether you want to do something about it.

1. Do you lose time from work due to your drinking?
2. Is drinking making your home life unhappy?
3. Do you drink because you are shy with other people?
4. Is drinking affecting your reputation?
5. Have you ever felt remorse after drinking?
6. Have you gotten into financial difficulties as a result of your drinking?
7. Do you turn to lower companions and an inferior environment when drinking?
8. Does your drinking make you careless of your family's welfare?
9. Has your ambition decreased since drinking?
10. Do you crave a drink at a definite time daily?
11. Do you want a drink the next morning?
12. Does drinking cause you to have difficulty in sleeping?
13. Has your efficiency decreased since drinking?
14. Is drinking jeopardizing your job or business?
15. Do you drink to escape from worries or troubles?
16. Do you drink alone?
17. Have you ever had a complete loss of memory as a result of your drinking?
18. Has your physician ever treated you for drinking?
19. Do you drink to build up your self-confidence?
20. Have you ever been in a hospital or institution on account of drinking?

(The above questions are used by many chemical dependency counselors, says the writer of them, in helping clients determine whether they have a problem with alcohol. In the pastoral counseling book mentioned above, The Rev. Dr. Howard Clinebell examined and reviewed several variations of the foregoing questions; so the particular question formats are not embedded in stone)

The Health and Human Services Guide. Then there's the recently published *Helping Patients Who Drink Too Much: A Clinicians Guide, 2005 Edition.* U.S. Department of Health and Human Services. It has all kinds of tests to aid physicians in diagnosis, evaluation, and treatment. And they are worth looking at. But the pamphlet is sadly lacking in applause for A.A. or in mention of cure by religious means.

4. **Requiring an admission of defeat**: Here were some comments that were common in the early days: "I am licked" (See Dick B., *The Akron Genesis of Alcoholics Anonymous*, 2d ed., pp. 256-257). "I had met my match. I had been overwhelmed. Alcohol was my master" (*Alcoholics Anonymous*, 4th ed., p. 8). There was often too a cry for help: "O God, manage me, because I can't manage myself" (See Dick B., *Anne Smith's Journal, 1933-1939*, 3rd ed, pp. 20-22).

5. **Step Zero—Is the newcomer willing to go to any lengths to get well—to quit drinking entirely:** See *Our Legacy to the Faith Community: A Twelve-Step Guide for Those Who Want to Believe*, written by three of Clarence Snyder Sponsee Old-timers and Their Wives (Winter Park FL: Came to Believe Publications, 2005, Compiled and Edited by Dick B., pp. 13-14). See also Dick B., *That Amazing Grace: The Role of Clarence and Grace S. in Alcoholics Anonymous*, pp. 65-66; and *Alcoholics Anonymous*, 4th ed., p. 58).

6. **Establishing and requiring the newcomer's belief in Yahweh, the Creator, our Almighty God.** Early AAs were not allowed to pussyfoot. They were asked fearlessly to "face the proposition that either God is everything or else He is nothing. God either is, or He isn't" (*Alcoholics Anonymous*, 4th ed, p. 53). There is almost an exact parallel between this Big Book phrase and the one used in books by Rev. Sam Shoemaker (See Samuel M. Shoemaker, Jr., *Confident Faith*, p. 187) AAs were to follow and believe **Hebrews 11:6:**

> But without faith it is impossible to please him: for he that cometh to God must believe that he is, and that he is a rewarder of them that diligently seek him.

There was an insistence that they believe that God is (See *DR. BOB and the Good Oldtimers*, p.144. See Samuel M. Shoemaker, Jr., *Religion That Works*, p. 88; *The Gospel According to You*, p. 47; *National Awakening*, p. 40—all referring to Hebrews 11:6 (Wilson wrote in *Alcoholics Anonymous*, 4th ed., at p. 57: "Even so has God restored us all to our right minds. . . He has come to all who have honestly sought Him. When we drew near to Him, He disclosed Himself to us!" and at page 62: "We had to have God's help").

7. Belief followed by requisite surrenders: No one was admitted to A.A. without undergoing a "real surrender." Sometimes part of it occurred at the time of his discharge from the hospital (See Dick B., *That Amazing Grace,* p. 26; *DR. BOB and the Good Oldtimers,* p. 144). But the "real surrender" occurred when he was taken upstairs at the Wednesday night meeting, got down on his knees, and had the "elders" pray over him after the manner of James 5:16. (Dick B., *That Amazing Grace, supra,* pp. 27-28; *When Early AAs Were Cured and Why,* pp. 100-101). The procedure usually involved these declarations and prayers:

> *I confess Jesus Christ as my Lord and Saviour*
>
> *I ask God in the name of Jesus Christ to take alcohol out of my life.*
>
> *And I ask for the strength and guidance to live by the cardinal principles taught by Jesus Christ, particularly those in the Four Absolutes—honesty, purity, unselfishness, and love.*

The general form, content, and existence of these surrenders is well documented history. Regrettably indeed, it is just seldom discussed. See Dick B., *The James Club, supra,* pp. 155-157, 166; *The Golden Text of A.A.,* p. 32; *When Early AAs Were Cured and Why,* pp. 100-101; *That Amazing Grace,* pp. 27, 72-73; Mitch K., *How It Worked,* pp. 58, 70; Samuel M. Shoemaker, Jr., *The Experiment of Faith,* pp. 27-29).

8. The necessity for learning about and standing with the full armour of God:

> "Finally, my brethren, be strong in the Lord, and in the power of his might. Put on the whole armour of God, that ye may be able to stand against the wiles of the devil. For we wrestle not against flesh and blood, but against principalities, against powers, against the rulers of the darkness of this world, against spiritual wickedness in high places. Wherefore take unto you the whole armour of God, that ye may be able to withstand

in the evil day, and having done all, to stand" (Ephesians 6:10-13).

Most of the remaining verses in Ephesians 6 describe in battle figures of speech: standing on truth, righteousness, the gospel of peace, the shield of faith, the helmet of salvation, the sword of the Spirit, which is the word of God, and praying.)

The pioneers heard additional calls to stand and resist:

> "Submit yourselves therefore to God. Resist the devil, and he will flee from you. . . . Humble yourselves in the sight of the Lord, and he shall lift you up" (James 4:7, 10)

> "Blessed is the man that endureth temptation: for when he is tried, he shall receive the crown of life which the Lord hath promised to them that love him. . . . Do not err, my beloved brethren" (James 1:12, 16)

9. Obeying God's commandments—seeking and doing:

> "But seek ye first the kingdom of God and his righteousness, and all these things will be added unto you" (Matthew 6:33).

> "But be ye doers of the word, and not hearers only, deceiving your own selves" (James 1:22)

> "Thy will be done" (Matthew 6:10)

> Love God with all your heart, soul, and strength, and your neighbor as yourself (Matthew 22:36-40)

> "For this is the love of God, that we keep his commandments; and his commandments are not grievous" (1 John 5:3).

"Owe no man any thing, but to love one another: for he that loveth another hath fulfilled the law" (Romans 13:8)

"Let love be without dissimulation. Abhor that which is evil; cleave to that which is good" (Romans 12:9),

9. Growing in the relationship with the Father and His Son

Walk in fellowship: "And these things write we unto you, that your joy may be full. This then is the message which we have heard of him, and declare unto you, that God is light, and in him is no darkness at all. If we say that we have fellowship with him, and walk in darkness, we lie, and do not the truth. But if we walk in the light, as he is in the light, we have fellowship one with another, and the blood of Jesus Christ his son cleanseth us from all sin" (1 John 1:4-7)

Study the Bible: "Study to shew thyself approved unto God a workman that needeth not to be ashamed, rightly dividing the word of truth" (2 Timothy 2:15)

Prayer and thanksgiving: "Pray without ceasing. In every thing give thanks: for this is the will of God in Christ Jesus concerning you" (1 Thessalonians 5:17-18)

Ask God for wisdom: "If any of you lack wisdom, let him ask of God. That giveth to all men liberally, and upbraideth not; and it shall be given him" (James 1:5)

Forgiving: "Forbearing one another, and forgiving one another, if any man have a quarrel against any: even as Christ forgave you; so also do ye" (Colossians 3:13)

Using "helpful books" such as *The Upper Room*, *The Runner's Bible*, *The Greatest Thing in the World*, *The Meaning of Prayer*, Glenn Clark books, E. Stanley

Jones books, Emmet Fox books. Books on love, prayer, healing, the life of Jesus Christ, and—of course—the Bible.

10. Witnessing:

Working with other alcoholics: "Practical experience shows that nothing will so much insure immunity from drinking as intensive work with other alcoholics" (*Alcoholics Anonymous*, 4th ed., p. 89. Dick B.: Yet how often we see members fervently attending meetings, "serving," speaking, enjoying conferences—and yet never working directly with and helping the newcomer. In my own case, after more than nineteen years of sobriety, I still remember and try to practice which Bill W. and Dr. Bob preached on this newcomer matter)

You have to give it away to keep it. "And he said unto them, Go ye into all the world, and preach the gospel to every creature. He that believeth and is baptized shall be saved; but he that believeth not shall be damned. And these signs shall follow them that believe. . ." (Mark 16:15-17; and see Dick B., *Anne Smiths Journal, supra*, pp. 65, 69, 73, 87, 88, 124, 140; Samuel M. Shoemaker, Jr., *They're on the Way*, p. 159; *One Boy's Influence,* p. 15)

Go and tell what God has done: "Jesus answered and said unto them. Go and shew John again those things which you do hear and see: The blind receive their sight, and the lame walk, the lepers are cleansed, and the deaf hear, the dead are raised up, and the poor have the gospel preached to them" (Matthew 11:4-5; Dick B.: Get the message straight. The first message Bill W. ever heard was from his friend Ebby who said: "I've got religion. . . .[and then Ebby] made the point blank declaration that God had done for him what he could not do for himself. His human will had failed. Doctors had pronounced him incurable. Society was about to lock him up" *Alcoholics Anonymous*, 4th ed., pp. 9, 11.

The message was not "Don't drink and go to meetings." It was in effect: Look what you have seen in me. And it is God who deserves the glory. Rev. Sam Shoemaker put it more eloquently by suggesting "Marvel at what God has done for you." Shoemaker, *If I Be Lifted Up*, pp. 13, 84, 141) That sharing of what God has done and giving Him the credit, said Sam. is what strangely warms the hearts; Shoemaker, *National Awakening*, p. 28).

11. Walking in Love and Service:

The United Christian Endeavor Society of Dr. Bob's youth stressed "love and service" as its theme. And years later, Dr. Bob declared that the Twelve Steps, when simmered to their essence, amounted to "love and service." Dick B. *The James Club*, pp. 142, 154-155.

"Walk in love," declares the Word. And he that is "chiefest," says the Word, is he who must serve others. Strong verses about these two principles are:

> *Love*: "Be ye therefore followers of God as dear children. And walk in love, as Christ also hath loved us, and hath given himself for us as an offering and sacrifice to God for a sweetsmelling savour" (Ephesians 5:1-2)

> *Serve*: "But so shall it not be among you: but whosoever will be great among you, shall be your minister: And whosoever of you will be the chiefest, shall be servant of all. For even the Son of man came not to be ministered to, but to minister, and to give his life a ransom for many" (Mark 10:43-44; Dick B.: This was a favorite quote by Dr. Bob, pointing to the humility needed in helping others. Wilson put the following in his Tradition Two: "For our group purpose there is but one ultimate authority—a loving God as He may express Himself in our group conscience. Our leaders are but trusted servants; they do not govern." *Alcoholics Anonymous*, 4th ed, p. 562)

12. Fellowship with like-minded believers:

"That which we have seen and heard declare we unto you, that ye also may have fellowship with us: and truly our fellowship Is with the Father, and with his Son Jesus Christ" (1John 1:3)

"And they continued stedfastly in the apostles' doctrine and fellowship, and in breaking of bread, and in prayers" (Acts 2:42)

"Be ye not unequally yoked together with unbelievers: for what fellowship hath righteousness with unrighteousness? And what communion hath light with darkness? And what concord hath Christ with Belial? And what part hath he that believeth with an infidel? And what agreement hath the temple of God with idols? For ye are the temple of the living God; as God hath said, I will dwell in them, and walk in them; and I will be their God, and they shall be my people. Wherefore come out from among them, and be ye separate, saith the Lord, and touch not the unclean thing; and I will receive you" (2 Corinthians 6:14-17. Dick B.: Some things Christians might think about useful senses-knowledge thoughts in A.A. itself: (a) Stay away from slippery places and slippery people. (b) If you go into a barbershop, expect to get a haircut. (c) Frequently meetings are described as "Centers for Self-centeredness," "Relationships Anonymous," and "Alcoholics Monotonous," where the talk is all about fear, sexual r relationships, daily problems, misery, suffering, and failures. Whether you regard such meetings as appropriate in the A.A. light, or whether you regard them as feeding-troughs of unbelief, negative ideas, Christian-bashing, or despair, you'll get very little profit or support or Biblical fortification by chumming around in them. Or with the people who keep offering human negativity instead of Christian victory. One archivist suggested: Stay away from "group depression meetings." In difficult King's English, 2 Corinthians 10:5 says:

Casting down imaginations, and every high thing that exalteth itself against the knowledge of God, and bringing into captivity every thought to the obedience of Christ.

Better to vote with your feet! Unless you are there to snag and rescue a newcomer. But go where believers go, read what they read, say what they say, do what they do, and ignore the company of naysayers. Those of my sponsees who embraced A.A. and didn't reject it, but who also welcomed fellowship with believers had an enviable record of positive success in A.A. and in attaining the abundant life that Jesus came to provide— John 10:10)

12. **Attend church or Bible studies and fellowships.**

If you want to stick with the pioneer winners and do what their leader Dr. Bob did, you'll recognize the importance he placed on attending church in sobriety. Also, his repeated stress on Bible study and prayer. Even in the Big Book, Bill Wilson wrote: "Not all of us join religious bodies, but most of us favor such memberships" (*Alcoholics Anonymous*, 4th ed., p. 28). At page 87, Wilson also suggested in his Eleventh Step discussion: "There are many helpful books also. Suggestions about these may be obtained from one's priest, minister, or rabbi. Be quick to see where religious people are right. Make use of what they offer" (p. 87).

In early A.A., there was no endorsement of any particular sect or denomination. Neither was there any ballyhoo against them, like that you sometimes hear today. Similarly, A.A. was aligned with no particular church, sect, or denomination and hence kept the doors open to all even in the founding days—to the point that, when Cleveland Roman Catholics were having difficulty with the Akron Protestant leanings, they followed the lead of the non-Roman Catholic old-timer Clarence Snyder and formed the first A.A. group consisting of alcoholics only—in Cleveland. Remember too that they took with them to their Cleveland fellowship the Bible and the teachings of Jesus in the "Four Absolutes" *in toto*

13. **Recognizing that the early AAs had as their objective the cure of alcoholism by the Creator**, about which the three earliest members spoke so much (See *Alcoholics Anonymous*, 4th ed., p. 191; Dick B., *The Golden Text of A.A.; Cured: Proven Help for Alcoholics and Addicts*).

2

The Healing Evidence at the Time When A.A. Was Born

Miracles Never Ceased

The extensive records of Divine healing through the ages: The record of healing approaches that relied on God and took their facts from the Bible has simply blasted unbelieving A.A. revisionists out of the water when that record is compared to their self-help and self-made spirituality themes.

These people either don't know or don't want to get into the hefty volumes about signs, miracles, wonders, and cures by the power of God. There are volumes of recorded histories of healings that: (1) begin in the Old Testament, (2) continue through the healings by Jesus, (3) were wrought by the Apostles and early Christians as recorded in the Book of Acts; (4) continued with the Church Fathers and then (5) on down through the ages.

See Herbert Lockyear, *All the Miracles of the Bible: The Supernatural in Scripture—Its Scope and Significance.* Grand Rapids, MI: Zondervan Pubishing House, 1961; G. H. R. Shafto. *The Wonders of The Kingdom: A Study of the Miracles of Jesus.* New York: George H. Doran Company, 1924; Morton T. Kelsey. *Psychology, Medicine & Christian Healing: A Revised and Expanded Edition of Healing & Christianity.* San Francisco: Harper & Row, Publishers, 1988; Pearcy Dearmer. *Body and Soul: An Enquiry Into The Effects of Religion Upon Health, With a Description of Christian Works of Healing From the New Testament to the Present Day.* London: Sir Isaac Pitman & Sons, 1909; J. R. Pridie. *The Church's Ministry of Healing.* London: Society for Promoting Chistian Knowledge, 1926; F. W. Puller. *Anointing of the Sick In Scripture and Tradition With Some Consideration of the Numbering of the Sacraments.* London: Society For Promoting Christian Knowledge, 1904; and C.S. Lewis. *Miracles:*

How God Intervenes in Nature and Human Affairs. New York: Collier Books, 1960.

One of the best and most comprehensive renditions of my own research work on this subject was included in the address I gave at The Second Nationwide Alcoholics Anonymous History Conference in Wilmington, Delaware. And after the conference, I revised the materials and did an immense amount of additional research. You can find it in my new title Dick B. *When Early AAs Were Cured and Why. 3rd ed.* Kihei, HI: Paradise Research Publications, Inc., 2006. In Appendix Three of that title is my documentation with the title "Miracles Not to Be Forgotten" at pages 143 to 159. There is also an extensive Bibliography in the title.

Recognition of the Efficacy of Healings

The Remarks of Clergy at Yale Summer School of Alcohol Studies about the efficacy of divine healing of alcoholism: The foregoing material was available and discussed, though probably ignored, when the A.A. program was being launched. Dr. Bob certainly studied these matters extensively as a reading of the books in his library quickly shows. And at the very conference where Bill Wilson was in attendance and speaking, scholars were making the following statements. The specifics are laid out in my title *When Early AAs Were Cured, supra,* pp. 1-3.

The remarks are those of Reverend Francis W. McPeek, Executive Director of the Federation of Churches in Washington, D.C. and of The Reverend Dr. Otis R. Rice, Director, St. Luke's Hospital, New York. First, from Rev. McPeek's comments:

> It is, moreover, the insistence of historical Christianity that no man can live fully without a knowledge of and dependence upon God. . . . No one is exempt.
>
> The deep-running for a faith which united and heals the soul and directs the will, and the bits of emotionally tinged knowledge of God from earlier times, are activated in many ways. . . . Augustine was converted

by reading a single passage. St. Anthony by a single word.

Much work was done in city missions and particularly by the Salvation Army. . . . Generally speaking, the Salvationists have capitalized on the techniques that have made other reform programs work.

[Early AAs were pointed to the best-selling book by Harold Begbie *Twice-Born Men* that described the Salvationist work in the London slums. As summarized by Rev. McPeek, those techniques were:] (1) Insistence on abstinence [the primary rule for A.A. pioneers]. (2) reliance on God [the first test required by Dr. Bob as newcomers left the hospital] (3) the provision of new friendships among those who understand [the social and religious comradeship that was part of the pioneer program] (4) the opportunity to work with those who suffer from the same difficulty [the love and service to other alcoholics that was, as Dr. Bob expressed it, the essence of the new ideas in A.A.] (5) unruffled patience and consistent faith in the ability of the individual and in the power of God to accomplish the desired ends [The whole Akron program involved living in the homes of people like Bob and Anne Smith, having Quiet Time, reading Christian literature, and engaging in ceaseless conversions, Bible study, prayer, fellowship, and witness].

Continuing his comments to the Yale Audience, Rev. McPeek said:

Certain things may be held as conclusive. Towering above them all is **this indisputable fact: It is faith in the living God which has accounted for more recoveries from the disease than all other therapeutic agencies put together.**

And then from the Reverend Dr. Rice to the Yale Summer School:

It is from the fact that one is a miserable sinner, and the acceptance of the fact that by God's promise one can become His son, that cures are made and that lives are made worthwhile.

Healing Assurances pioneer AAs heard and studied in the Bible itself and in verses from it:

There are enough verses the AAs studied in the Bible on healing to keep you busy reading for weeks, and the following are neither exhaustive nor complete. They simply show a little of what God had to say as He spoke through His Word. They also show what early AAs were regularly hearing, studying and believing. We know this because we know that the devotionals they used daily contained these very verses. See Nora Holm. *The Runner's Bible* (reprinted) Lakewood, Co: Acropolis Books, 1998, pp. 171-196. Also the many verses in the Methodist Quarterly the *Upper Room*, which was given to every one of the pioneers. And in the many healing books studied and circulated by Dr. Bob to the pioneer AAs and their families. See Dick B., *Dr. Bob and His Library, 3rd ed.* Kihei, HI: Paradise Research Publications, Inc., 1998, pp. 35-40, 83-89; *Cured: Proven Help for Alcoholics and Addicts*, Paradise, *supra*; *God and Alcoholism*, Paradise, *supra*..

Verses In the Old Testament:

> . . . I am the LORD [Yahweh] that healeth thee (Exodus 15:26b)

> . . . Thus saith the LORD, the God of David thy father. I have heard thy prayer. I have seen thy tears. Behold, I will heal thee. . . (2 Kings 20:5)

> Bless the LORD, O my soul. . . . Who forgiveth all thine I niquities, who healeth all thy diseases (Psalm 103:1, 3)

> Then they cry unto the LORD in their trouble, and he saves them out of their distresses. He sent his word and healed them (Psalm 107:19-20)

> I have seen his ways and will heal him (Isaiah 57:18)

> For I will restore health unto thee, and I will heal thee of thy wounds, saith the LORD (Jeremiah 30:17)

Verses in the Gospels:

And in that same hour he [Jesus] cured many of their infirmities and plagues, and of evil spirits; and unto many that were blind he gave sight (Luke 7:21)

Jesus saith unto him, Rise, take up thy bed, and walk. And immediately the man was made whole, and took up his bed, and walked. . . (John 5:8-10; compare *Alcoholics Anonymous*, 4th ed, p. 19)

[After he had cured many of their infirmities and given sight to the blind] . . . Jesus answering said unto them, Go your way, and tell John what things ye have seen and heard; how that the blind see, the lame walk, the lepers are cleansed, the deaf hear, the dead are raised, to the poor the gospel is preached (Matthew 7:22)

And when he [Jesus] had called unto him his twelve disciples, he gave them power against unclean spirits, to cast them out, and to heal all manner of sickness, and all manner of disease (Matthew 10:1)

After these things the Lord appointed other seventy also, and sent them two and two before his face into every city and place, whither he himself would come. Therefore he said unto them. . . . And heal the sick that are therein, and say unto them. The kingdom of God is come nigh unto you (Luke 10:1-2, 9)

Verily, verily, I say unto you, He that believeth on me, the works that I do shall he do also; and greater works than these shall he do; because I go unto my Father (John 14:12)

[After the apostles and others had seen Jesus risen from the dead following his resurrection, Peter preached as follows:] How God anointed Jesus of Nazareth with the Holy Ghost and power, who went about doing good, and healing all that were oppressed of the devil; for

God was with him. And we are witnesses of all things which he did both in the land of the Jews, and in Jerusalem. . . .(Acts 10:38-39).

And then among the many verses, after the Gospels:

"And by the hands of the apostles were many signs and wonders wrought among the people; (and they were all with one accord in Solomon's porch. . . . And believers were the more added to the Lord, multitudes both of men and women. Insomuch that they brought forth the sick into the streets, and laid them on beds and couches, that at least the shadow of Peter passing by might overshadow some of them. There came also a multitude out of the cities round about unto Jerusalem, bringing sick folks, and them which were vexed with unclean spirits; and they were healed every one" (Acts 5:12, 14-16)

Were and are the records AAs studied on divine healing of any relevance to the cures early AAs claimed?

- **The real question here is whether – seventy-five years after the founding of the A.A. Society - we can say that A.A. has developed a program of complete recovery (Let's get bold and say, as Bill W., Dr. Bob, and Bill D. said it, a "cure") for those afflicted with alcoholism.**

    The answer will depend on several factors: What is alcoholism? What is the meaning of "recovery" and of "cure?" What were the ingredients of our original program? Was it dependent upon God? What God are we talking about? What answers were given by our founders and pioneers? What was the real success rate? How important is that history? Can we apply the answers to the cure of alcoholism in today's A.A.

- **It sums up this way: have we really got something to share about early A.A. and Christianity with others today? If so, what is it that we can share? And let's start with what A.A.'s own literature told us several decades ago:**

When Bill left Akron in late August 1935, there were four members–possibly five counting Phil, who might have been in the process of drying out. From that fall to spring, Bill helped Hank P. and Fitz M., among others, get sober in New York. He made a short visit to Akron in April, 1936, writing Lois that he had spent the weekend and was "so happy about everything there. Bob and Anne and Henrietta Seiberling have been working so hard with those men and with really wonderful success. There were very joyous get-togethers at Bob's, Henrietta's, and the Williams's by turns." In September 1936, there was another visit, with Bill's arrival "a signal for a house party, which was very touching," he wrote. "Anne and Bob and Henrietta have done a great job. There were several new faces since spring." In February 1937, another count was taken, and there were seven additional members in Akron, for a total of 12. Half of these had or would have some sort of slip, and at least one would never be really successful in the A.A. program thereafter. For most, however, the slip was a convincer. There were dozens of others who were exposed to the program up to February 1937. Some were successful for a time, then drifted away. Some came back. Others died. Some, like "Lil," may have found another way [*DR. BOB and the Good Oldtimers.* NY: Alcoholics Anonymous World Services, Inc., 1980, pp. 108-09]. Word of Akron's "not-drinking-liquor club" had already spread to nearby towns, such as Kent and Canton, and it was probably early 1937 when a few prospects started drifting down from Cleveland. In the beginning, it was in twos and threes (By 1939, there were two carloads) [*DR. BOB, supra*, p. 122]

In November of that year [1937], Bill Wilson went on a business trip that enabled him to make a stopover in Akron. . . . Bill's writings record the day he sat in the living room with Doc, counting the noses of our recoveries. "A hard core of very grim, last-gasp cases had by then been sober a couple of years, an unheard of development," he said. "There were twenty or more such people. All told, we figured that upwards of 40 alcoholics were staying bone dry." As we carefully rechecked this score, Bill said, it suddenly burst upon us that a new light was shining into the dark world of the alcoholic. . . . a "chain reaction" had started, and "Conceivably it could one day circle the whole world. . . . We actually wept for joy," Bill said, "and Bob and Anne and I bowed our heads in silent thanks" [*DR. BOB, supra,* p 123].

"A beacon had been lighted. God had shown alcoholics how it might be passed from hand to hand. Never shall I forget that great and humbling hour of realization, shared with Dr. Bob," said Bill [*RHS*, p. 8].

- **The founders' elation over successes was more than justified and confirmed by the careful investigation of Frank Amos and reported to John D. Rockefeller, Jr. in 1938.** Frank Amos gave Rockefeller a glowing report about Dr. Bob and Akron's Group Number One that had caught Mr. Rockefeller's interest and had further encouraged the formation of the Alcoholic Foundation. And Frank Amos has left us with a detailed description of the program as it stood before the writing of the Big Book began. Bill began writing the Big Book in 1938. According to his secretary, Nell Wing, there were slightly more than 70 alcoholics that had achieved sobriety. There never were the "100 men and women" that Bill mentioned when the Big Book was published in the Spring of 1939. Of those who were sober, fifty percent had maintained continuous sobriety; twenty-five percent had achieved sobriety after relapse; and the remainder "showed improvement." These were the people who "really tried," to use Bill's terms; and we have no doubt that there were many other "rim-runners" who came and went but simply never made the cut. By the early 1940's, records in Cleveland showed that 93 percent of those who came to A.A. never had a drink again [*DR. BOB*, *supra*, p. 261].

And now for the history to be taught, learned, known, and passed along.

3

Alcoholics Anonymous, the Founders, Belief in Almighty God and Divine Healing

Without Any Apparent Exception, A.A.'s Founders Believed the Creator Cured Them

The Founders and Early A.A. Writings and Statements: There is no need here to go to the documentation in my titles *God and Alcoholism: Our Growing Opportunity in the 21st Century; Cured: Proven Help for Alcoholics and Addicts;* and *When Early AAs Were Cured and Why.* Suffice it to say that Bill Wilson said the Lord had cured him of his "terrible disease." Dr. Bob spoke of Wilson's being cured and then told the staff at his hospital that he and another [Wilson] had discovered a cure for alcoholism. A.A. Number Three, Bill Dotson, declared that Wilson's statement that the Lord had cured him had become for him [Dotson] the golden text of A.A. (See Dick B., *The Golden Text of A.A.*)

The Pioneer Members: Early Pioneer member Clarence Snyder spoke many times of the cures early AAs had received. See Mitch K., *How It Worked*. It's not accidental that the person who drafted one of the proposed covers for the First Edition of *Alcoholics Anonymous* (published in 1939) put the following in prominent print on the cover: **"Alcoholics Anonymous: Their Pathway to a Cure."** Wilson and Hank Parkhurst were so convinced of their cure for alcoholism that they prepared an outline of their new book whose title page read: **"Alcoholics Anonymous Published by Alcoholics Anonymous, Inc. A Non Profit Organization for the Promotion of Cure and Understanding of Alcoholism."** Extensive remarks of this kind were made by Larry Jewell (who was sponsored by Dr. Bob and Clarence Snyder). Jewell made them in a series of articles he wrote for *The*

Houston Press in 1940. And the words of these old timers were echoed by others contemporaneously. The Reverend Dr. Dilworth Lupton, pastor of the First Unitarian Church in Cleveland, wrote of the new cure in the *Cleveland Plain Dealer* in 1939. Morris Markey spoke of the "miraculous" "cure" for habitual drunkards in his *Liberty Magazine* article in 1939. Theodore English wrote in *Scribner's Commentator* in January of 1941 that Wilson had developed a cure that had enlisted half the alcoholics encountered by the Houston AA group and cured two-thirds of them. Dr. William Duncan Silkworth (who wrote the "Doctor's Opinion" for *Alcoholics Anonymous*) told one of his alcoholic patients (Charles K.) that the only hope for his cure was through the "Great Physician," Jesus Christ. See Norman Vincent Peale, *The Positive Power of Jesus Christ* (NY: Guideposts, 1980), pp. 59-63 and Dale Mitchel. *Silkworth The Little Doctor Who Loved Drunks: The Biography of William Duncan Silkworth, M.D.* Center City, MN: Hazelden, 2002, pp. 46-51. Writing in 1939, Silkworth had buttressed the new approach by Wilson's A.A. by saying:

> **That the chronic alcoholic has sometimes recovered by religious means is a fact centuries old**. But these recoveries have been sporadic, insufficient in numbers or impressiveness to make headway with the alcoholic problem as a whole (Mitchel, *Silkworth, supra*, p. 159, bold face added)

A.A.'s own publication: Finally, the *AA Grapevine* published an article by the famous medical writer Paul de Kruif stating the "A.A.'s medicine is God and God alone. This is their discovery... [and] that the patients it cures have to nearly die before they can bring themselves to take it."

The Recent Surveys after 2000 by Richard K. I will not go into further details about what happened when the A.A. Christian Fellowship tackled the problem because Richard K. (a young investigative reporter, researcher, and A.A. member in Massachusetts) has done a masterful job of documenting hundreds and hundreds of contemporary statements—by early AAs, by newspapers, by magazines, and in A.A.'s own scrap books at World Headquarters—that AAs all over the United States were being cured of Alcoholism.

This research and these records should not go unexamined and ignored by those who want to know if there is proof of early A.A. cures. See Richard K. *New Freedom: Reclaiming Alcoholics Anonymous, 2005 Manuscript,* consisting of more than 500 pages that are carefully presented, documented in detail with extensive footnotes, and include an extensive bibliography.

In Appendix I, Richard compiled and presented the most detailed and thoroughly documented study of the early A.A. pioneers and their recovery histories. The appendix is titled, *"A New Light: The First Forty": A Chronological Survey of the Early A.A. Pioneers" (December 1934-1939),* pp. 379-389.

In Appendix II, Richard offers his *"Diary of a Cure (A Documented Chronology of A.A.'s Cure for Al*coholism)." His detailed items can be found at pp. 391-434 of *New Freedom,* supra.
This 2005 effort follows equally probative works by Richard K.

The *New Freedom* piece follows three other scholarly works on the subject by Richard K. *A New Light: The First Forty – A Chronological survey of the Early A.A. Pioneers (1934-1939),* Haverhill, MA: Golden Text Publishing Company, 2003; *Early A.A. – Separating Fact from Fiction: How Revisionists Have Led Our History Astray,* Golden Text Publishing, *supra,* 2003; *So You Think Drunks Can't Be Cured? – Press Releases By Witnesses to the Cure.* Golden Text Publishing, supra, 2003.

I will be so bold as the suggest that no one who, beginning about the year 2000, writes about or researches the history of A.A. should be able to hold his head above water if he has not examined these historical accounts by Richard K., by Dale Mitchel, by Mitch K., and by myself.

The Dramatic Denial in Later A.A.

"Once an alcoholic always an alcoholic!" Right? No. Wrong! By 1980--forty-five years after A.A.'s founding--an AA "Conference Approved" publication presumed to say out of thin air and yet quite bluntly that, in effect, the countless statements in A.A. and elsewhere were mistaken, misleading, and wrong [*DR. BOB, supra,* p. 136]. Despite this about-face by official A.A. employees, the only bases for such a claim that the founders had misrepresented to, and mislead the facts to the world were two ideas Bill Wilson had inserted in his Big Book four years *after* A.A.'s founding. Yet these negative and uncorroborated denials have persisted through all four editions of A.A.'s basic text. These new ideas were: (1) "We have seen the truth demonstrated again and again: 'Once an alcoholic always an alcoholic'." (*Alcoholics Anonymous*, 4th ed., p. 33). (2) "We are not cured of alcoholism" (*Alcoholics Anonymous*, 4th ed., p. 85).

The first statement, according to Wilson's own explicit admission, came from a contemporary therapist named Richard R. Peabody, who died drunk, and therefore "proved," said Wilson, that alcoholism was "uncurable." The second statement flew in the face of all the evidence we cited above, which demonstrates that alcoholics *had* been cured, that they had been cured by God, and that the cures were miraculous, astonishing, and the basis for the whole "spiritual program of recovery" that AAs developed between 1935 and 1938. Details and documentation for each of these points can be found in Dick B., *Cured: Proven Help for Alcoholics and Addicts* (Kihei, HI: Paradise Research Publications, Inc., 2003); Richard R. Peabody, *The Common Sense of Drinking* (Atlantic Monthly Press Book, 1933); and Katherine McCarthy, *The Emanuel Movement and Richard Peabody* (Journal of Studies on Alcohol, Vol. 45, No. 1, 1984).

Once again: What happened to the large dose of Pre-A.A. miraculous healings by the power of God to which AAs were exposed?

Many have minimized or just plain dismissed the miraculous outright. They have done so in various ways, depending upon the era involved.

For example, Old Testament signs and wonders are often relegated to the myth bin by calling them interpretative, artistic, imaginative, embellished, "touched up, filled with discrepancies, or the products of tradition rather than experience." See Bernard W. Anderson, *Understanding The Old Testament* (NJ: Prentice-Hall, Inc., 1957), pp. 43-44, 180-82, 227, 385, 407-09. Other authorities, however, plainly state that signs, wonders, and miracles of Old Testament accounts had as their object the indication of the severity of an illness and the gravity of the prognosis against which to contrast the greatness of the cure and the divine power that effected it. These authorities–and they are numerous—generally attribute the healings and miracles to the intervention of God. See *New Bible Dictionary, Second Edition* (England: Inter-Varsity Press, 1982), pp. 457-465:

The healing accounts of the Gospels have also been denied for a variety of reasons. Philip Schaff wrote: "The credibility of the Gospels would never have been denied if it were not for the philosophical and dogmatic skepticism which desires to get rid of the supernatural and miraculous at any price." See Philip Schaff, *History of the Christian Church, Volume I*, 3rd Revision (Grand Rapids, MI: Wm B. Eerdman's Publishing Company, 1890), p. 589. Decades later, writers popular in the early A.A. days, were still disputing the miraculous. See Emmet Fox, *The Sermon on the Mount* (New York: Harper & Row, 1934) and Dilworth Lupton, *Religion Says You Can* (Boston: The Beacon Press, 1938). Long before these johnnie-come-latelies of the 1930's, however, scholars were citing emphatically: "great writers who were by no means biased in favor of orthodoxy" [including] Dr. W.E. Channing, leader of American Unitarianism, who said: 'I know of no histories to be compared with the Gospels in marks of truth, in pregnancy of meaning, in quickening power. . . As to his [Christ's] biographers, they speak for themselves. Never were more simple and honest ones." Schaff, *History of the Christian Church*, *supra*, p. 589.

So, also, despite volumes of testimony to the contrary, writers and various "historians" have disputed the miracles and healings by the Apostles as recorded in the Book of Acts. They have alleged that the "age of miracles" in the First Century passed out of the picture, sometimes allegedly because the miracles were merely a stage which God no longer needed, or that they were myth and error. See Adolf Harnack, *The Expansion of Christianity in the First Three Centuries*, Vol I (Eugene, OR: Wipf and Stock Publishers, 1998), pp. 121, 143, 180, 256-57, 268. The disputers have also placed in their disputed box, categorized, minimized, ridiculed, and often rejected endless numbers of Christian healers and healings from Mary Baker Eddy to Lourdes to Benny Hinn and Oral Roberts.

But, for the founders of A.A., the proof was in the pudding; and Dr. Bob read extensively about healing by the power of God. In fact, even a brief glance at the Christian healing literature of the 1930's–in A.A.'s founding years–will disclose a myriad of scholarly studies of God's healing power and healings in the physical, psychological, mental, devil spirit, and other realms. We have included many of these in our bibliography.

Let's Look at the Bible Early AAs Were Studying for Basic Ideas about Healing and Cure

- **What the Bible has to say about:**

Miraculous healings long before Christ: Morton T. Kelsey comments: "As we have already seen, in the Old Testament there was no question, in theory, that Yahweh could heal. In several places remarkable instances were recorded. See Morton T. Kelsey, *Psychology, Medicine & Christian Healing*. Rev. and exp. ed. (San Francisco: Harper & Row, Publishers, 1966), p. 33. Specific examples include children given to women who were barren (Genesis 18:10, 14; Judges 13:5, 24; 1 Samuel 1:19-20; 2 Kings 4:16-17); the healing of Miriam's leprosy (Numbers 12:1-15) and Naaman's leprosy (2 Kings 5:1-14); healing of Jeroboam's paralyzed hand (1 Kings 13:1-6); raising from the dead by Elijah (1 Kings 17:17-24) and by Elisha (2 Kings 4:1-37); salvation of the Israelites from the later plagues in Egypt (Numbers 21:6-9); and the miracles wrought by Moses (Exodus 7-17). See *New Bible Dictionary, supra*, pp. 462, 782-83; Kelsey, *Psychology, Medicine & Christian Healing, supra*, pp. 33-36; In *Healing: Pagan And Christian* (London: Society For Promoting Christian Knowledge, 1935), George Gordon Dawson opines: "The standpoint of the Old Testament, generally, is that good health results from holy living. It is a divine gift and the reward of loving service. Any cure of disease was regarded as a gift from Yahweh, and resulted from forgiveness. The sick person made his peace with Him by repentance, intercession and sacrifice. The right spiritual relationship was restored. The soul was at rest, and the inner life being calm the bodily symptoms disappeared" (p. 90). Alan Richardson writes: . . . in the Old Testament the historically decisive event, which became for the Hebrew mind, the symbol and type of all God's comings in history is the Miracle of the Red Sea. See Alan Richardson, *The Miracle Stories of the Gospels* (London: SCM Press Ltd, 1941), pp. 3-4.

Miracles in the Gospels: "they brought unto Him all that were sick and them that were possessed with demons, and He healed many that were sick with diverse diseases, and cast out many demons. . . He had healed many in so much that as many as had plagues pressed upon Him that they might touch Him." See Elwood Worcester, Samuel McComb, Isador H. Coriat, *Religion and Medicine* (NY: Moffat, Yard & Company, 1908), p. 345; Elwood Worcester and Samuel McComb, *The Christian Religion As A Healing Power* (NY: Moffat, Yard & Company, 1909), pp. 84-97; G. R. H. Shafto, *The Wonders of The Kingdom: A Study of the Miracles of Jesus* (NY: George H. Doran Company, 1924), pp. 8-9. Shafto calculated that there are some forty-two of the foregoing indirect references to miraculous action on the part of Jesus in the four Gospels. Kelsey concluded: ". . . we find that everywhere Jesus went he functioned as a religious healer. Forty-one distinct instances of physical and mental healing are recorded in the four gospels (there are seventy-two accounts in all, including duplications), but this by no means represents the total. Many of these references summarize the healings of large numbers of people." See Kelsey, *Psychology, Medicine & Christian Healing, supra,* pp. 42-47. Alan Richardson points out the high proportion of the Gospel tradition that is devoted to the subject of miracle (209 verses out of 666 in the Gospel of Mark). See Richardson, *The Miracle Stories, supra,* p. 36. There are over 20 specific accounts - some healed at a distance, some with a word, and some with physical contact and means: blindness, deafness; dumbness, leprosy, epilepsy, dropsy, uterine hemorrhage, Peter's mother-in-law and her fever–possibly malaria, Malcus' severed ear; the man with withered hand, the woman bent double with a "spirit of infirmity," three separate people resurrected from the dead; the man paralyzed for 38 years, demoniacal possession, and so on. Percy Dearmer reports there are forty-one instances of Christ's works of healing in the Gospels (*Body and Soul, below,* p. 142-46). Also the miracles of water converted to wine, stilling of a storm, supernatural catch of fish, multiplying food, walking on water, money from a fish, a fig tree dried up. See *New Bible Dictionary, supra,* pp. 462-63; Leslie D. Weatherhead, *Psychology, Religion and Healing* (NY: Abingdon-Cokesbury Press, 1951), pp. 29-69; Worcester, McComb, Coriat, *Religion and Medicine, supra,* pp. 338-68; Josh McDowell, *Evidence*

That Demands a Verdict: historical evidences for the Christian faith (Campus Crusade for Christ, Inc., 1973), pp. 128-31. Luke 7:21-22 state: "And in that same hour he cured many of their infirmities and plagues, and of evil spirits; and unto many that were blind he gave sight. Then Jesus answering said unto them, Go your way, and tell John what things ye have seen and heard; how that the blind see, the lame walk, the lepers are cleansed, the deaf hear, the dead are raised, to the poor the gospel is preached." For a survey of the evidence, see E. R. Micklem, *Miracles & The New Psychology: A Study in the Healing Miracles of the New Testament.* London: Oxford University Press, 1922.

Miracles in the Book of Acts in Apostolic times: "many wonders and signs were done by the apostles. . .by the hands of the apostles were many signs and wonders wrought among the people. . . . Stephen, full of grace and power, wrought great wonders and signs. . . [as to Philip in Samaria] many with unclean spirits and many that were palsied and lame. . . [as to Paul and Barnabus] speaking of the signs and wonders God had wrought among the gentiles by them. . . [as to healing activities of Paul on the island of Malta] The rest also who had diseases in the island came and were cured" See Weatherhead, *Psychology, Religion and Healing, supra,* pp. 70-72; Kelsey, *Psychology, Medicine And Christian Healing, supra,* pp. 83-102. More specifically, the lame man at the Gate Beautiful, patients cured by the shadow of Peter and handkerchiefs which had touched them; restoration of the sight of Saul by Ananias; Peter's healing Aenes of palsy; the paralytic healed by Paul at Lystra; the healing of Publius's father of fever and dysentery by Paul; Dorcas and Eutychus were raised from the dead; multiple healings; and two occasions where demons were cast out. *See New Bible Dictionary, supra,* pp. 462-64. Harnack summed up with this quotation from Hebrews 2:3-4: "How shall we escape, if we neglect so great salvation: which at the first began to be spoken by the Lord, and was confirmed unto us by them that heard him; God also bearing them witness, both with signs and wonders, and with divers miracles, and gifts of the Holy Ghost, according to his own will?" See Harnack, *The Expansion of Christianity in the First Three Centuries,* Vol. I, *supra,* pp. 250-73. There is a list of the specific miracles in the Acts of the Apostles. See Pearcy Dearmer, *Body and Soul: An Enquiry into the Effects of Religion upon Health, with a Description of Christian Works of*

Healing From the New Testament to the Present Day. London: Sir Isaac Pitman & Sons, Ltd., 1909, pp. 183-91.

Let's Look at the Believers Who Healed Throughout History

What Early Christians accomplished was much expected::

[See John 14:12-14] Verily, verily, I say unto you, He that believeth on me, the works that I do shall he do also; and greater works than these shall he do; because I go unto my Father.

And whatsoever ye shall ask in my name, that will I do, that the Father may be glorified in the Son.

If ye shall ask anything in my name, I will do it]

Miracles after apostolic times and in early **centuries:** There is evidence of Christian healing from these sources: Quadratus of Athens (AD 126 or 127); St. Justin Martyr (the philosopher martyred circa 163, AD 100-163); St. Irenaeus (Bishop of Lyons, A.D. 120-202); Origen of Alexandria (AD 185-253), Tertullian (AD 193-211), St. Hilarion (monk, AD 291-371); St. Parthenius (Bishop of Lampsacus, AD circa 335-355); St. Macarius of Alexandria and four other Monks (AD 375-390); St. Martin (Bishop of Tours, AD circa 395- 397); St. Ambrose of Milan (AD 340-397), St. Chrysostom (AD 347-407), St. Augustine (AD 354-430), St. Jerome (AD 340-420); St. Symeon Stylites (layman, AD 391-460); St. Eugendus, Abbot of a monastery near Geneva, AD 455-517); St. Caesarius (Bishop of Arles, 502-542); St. German (Bishop of Paris, circa AD 555-576); St. Laumer priest near Chartres, AD 548-651); St. Eustace (Abbot of Luxeuil, circa 614-625); St. Riemirus (abbot of a monastery in the diocese of Le Mans, circa 660-699); Sophronius (Patriarch of Jerusalem, AD 640); St. Cuthbert (Bishop of Lindisfarne, AD 635-687), and St. John of Beverley (by Bede AD 721). See Leslie D. Weatherhead, *Psychology, Religion, and Healing, supra,* pp. 76-84; Worcester, McComb and Coriat, *Religion and Medicine, supra.* p. 367; Worcester and McComb, *The Christian Religion as a Healing Power, supra,* p.95. In a monumental treatise based largely on the Book of James as it relates to healing and anointing, F. W. Puller says: "I think I have shown that from the time of the Apostles onwards, during the first seven centuries of our era, the custom of praying over sick people and anointing them with holy oil continued without any break. And there seems to me to be good reasons for believing that in many cases the petitions that were offered were granted and that the holy oil was used by God as a channel for conveying health to the sick persons." See F. W. Puller, *The Anointing of the Sick in Scripture and Tradition, with some Considerations on the Numbering of the Sacraments* (London: Society For Promoting Christian Knowledge, 1904), p. 188; Pearcy Dearmer, *Body and Soul, supra*. Kelsey points to the important study by Evelyn Frost. which covers the earliest records of the church after the New Testament, from about the years 100 to 250 [Evelyn Frost, *Christian Healing: A Consideration of the Place of Spiritual Healing in the Church of To-day in the Light of the Doctrine and Practice of the Ante-Nicene Church* (1940)]; and Kelsey says of the Frost study: "It shows clearly that the practices of healing described in the New Testament continued without interruption for the next two centuries." Kelsey, *Psychology, Medicine And Christian Healing, supra*, pp. 103-156.

Healing ministry by individuals from 1091 forward to the late 1800's: There is testimony of individual healers, who, with no psychological technique, but through their communion with Christ by His power, healed the sick: St. Bernard of Clairvaux (1091-1153); St. Francis of Assisi (1182-1226); St. Thomas of Hereford (1282-1303); St. Catherine of Siena (1347-1380), Martin Luther (1483-1546), St. Francis Xavier (1506-1552), St. Philip Neri (1515-1595); George Fox (1624-1691); John Wesley (1703-1791); Prince Alexander of Hohenlohe (1794-1849); Father Theobald Matthew (of Ireland, 1790-1856), Dorothea Trudel (from Zurich, 1813-1862); Pastor John Christopher Blumhardt (Lutheran pastor from Stuttgart,1805-1880); and Father John of Cronstadt (of the Orthodox Church of the East, 1829-1908). See Weatherhead, *supra*, p. 86; Worcester and McComb, *Religion and Medicine, supra*, p. 367; Dearmer, *Body and Soul, supra*, p. 278, 338-82. Kelsey, *Psychology, Medicine And Christian Healing, supra*, pp. 157-188.

The erroneous hypothesis that miracles ended in the First Century even though there is no Biblical authority for this proposition–for

***such a cessation would have been contrary to the promises of the Creator*:** There has come into the healing picture the widely believed, but undocumented, claim that the "age of miracles" ended because God no longer had use for them. First of all, the Creator's abilities did not cease; nor did the power that He made available through the accomplishments of Jesus Christ end. That power and the gifts of healing may actually have been little used or undeclared because of church wrangling, but the Bible assurances did not change. Despite an increasing separation between medical healing and religious healing during the first years of the nineteenth century, "Pentecostal Christianity" and the work of many individuals brought Biblical assurances to the practical fore. The individuals included Glenn Clark, Mary Baker Eddy, A. J. Gordon, Pearcy Dearmer, Agnes Sanford, Starr Daily, John and Ethel Banks, Oral Roberts, Ruth Carter Stapleton, and a number in the Roman Catholic Community. See Kelsey, *Psychology, Medicine and Christian Religion, supra,* pp. 186-284.

> Yahweh's promises in His Word have not changed: See Exodus 15:26: "I am the Lord that healeth thee;" Psalm 103:3-4: Yahweh our God forgives all our iniquities, heals all our diseases, and redeems our lives from destruction; Matthew 10:8: "Heal the sick, cleanse the lepers, raise the dead, cast out devils: freely ye have received, freely give;" Mark 16:19-30: "And these signs shall follow them that believe: In my name shall they cast out devils; they shall speak with new tongues. . . they shall lay hands on the sick, and they shall recover;" John 14:12: "Verily, verily, I say unto you, He that believeth on me, the works that I do shall he do allso; and greater works than these shall he do; because I go unto my Father."
>
> These and many other Bible assurances were the daily diet of early AAs and particularly Dr. Bob as he frequently used *The Runner's Bible* devotional.
>
> See the verses and comments in Nora Smith Holm, *The Runner's Bible: Spiritual Guidance for People On The Run* (Lakewood,CO:I-Level Acropolis Books,

Publisher, 1998), pp. 171-96. Also, J. R. Pridie, *The Church's Ministry of Healing* (London: Society For Promoting Christian Knowledge,1926); C. S. Lewis, *Miracles: How God Intervenes in Nature and Human Affairs* (NY: Collier Books, 1947); Friedrich Heiler, *Prayer: A Study in the History of Psychology and Religion* (Oxford: Oneworld, 1932); Jim Wilson, *Healing Through The Power of Christ* (Cambridge, England: James Clarke & Co., Ltd., 1946); Dawson, *Healing: Pagan and Christian*, 1935, *supra;* Philip Inman, *Christ in the Modern Hospital* (London: Hodder & Stoughton Limited, 1937); G. R. H. Shafto, *The Wonders of the Kingdom*, 1924, *supra*.

- **The Successes of the Christian Missions and Evangelism**:

A. Rescue Missions: Religious "conversion" was the catchword for such endeavors, but this kind of language masked the importance of the Creator, the place of Jesus Christ, and the use of the Bible, prayer, and healing. It is quite fair to say that the latter–the Creator, Jesus Christ, Bible, prayer, and healing, rather than "conversion"–marked the mission and program of the missions. See the excellent survey in: Howard Clinebell, *Understanding and Counseling Persons with Alcohol, Drug, and Behavioral Addictions*. Rev. and Enl. Ed. Nashville: Abingdon Press, 1968, pp. 167-194.The following were the three major mission landmarks:

(1) Jerry McCauley's Water Street Mission was founded in October, 1872 - the outcropping of his own deliverance from alcoholism; and it helped thousands. Meetings were simple. There were no sermons. They opened with singing, a Bible reading, and a message from Jerry. This was followed by testimonies where drunkards spoke of their fall and rebirth. Often, Jerry laid hands on the penitent and encouraged him to pray out loud for himself.

(2) Next came the Gospel Missions - still in existence today with a new name, but better remembered as the International Union of Gospel Missions. In April, 1882, Samuel Hadley overcame his alcoholism with a religious experience and passed the Gospel mission torch to his son, and these events marked the beginning of that approach.

(3) Hadley's son later was in charge of Calvary Rescue Mission with Shoemaker being an underlying recovery force when Sam became rector of Calvary Episcopal Church in New York in 1925. It was through decisions for Christ at the Calvary Rescue Mission that Ebby Thacher, Bill Wilson, and thousands of others soon overcame their alcoholism. The meetings involved hymns, Bible reading, prayers, testimonies, and decisions for Christ. The cry was "I've got religion." (William L. White. *Slaying the Dragon: The History of Addiction Treatment and Recovery in America.* Bloomington, IL: Chestnut Health Systems/Lighthouse Institute, 1998, pp. 71-74). Reverend Shoemaker uttered a simple description of Calvary's Mission on November 25, 1932. He said it was "where God reclaims men who choose to be reborn." See Dick B. *Turning Point: A History of Early A.A.'s Spiritual Roots and Successes.* Kihei, HI: Paradise Research Publications, Inc., 1997, p. 96.

B. The Salvation Army: It was founded in 1865 out of the pastoral work of a Methodist Minister William Booth. It was first called the Christian Revival Association and rechristened the Salvation Army in 1878. Its vision was that Christian salvation and moral education in a wholesome environment would save the body and soul of the alcoholic. There were so many cures that the Salvation Army served alcoholics for more than a century and was called "the largest and most successful rehabilitation program for transient alcoholic men in the United States." Its most striking testimonials were those in Harold Begbie's *Twice Born Men* - about rescue in the slums of London. This was a book widely read by A.A. pioneers and recommended by Dr. Bob's wife Anne. And it is important to understand the emphasis on conversion that Harold Begbie repeatedly makes with reference to the Salvation Army. Though he was probably too much influenced by Professor James' definition of conversion, Begbie nonetheless quotes with favor the following American writer who was actually quoted by James himself:

> I am bold to say that the work of God in the conversion of one soul, considered together with the source, foundation, and purchase of it, and also the benefit and eternal issue of it, is a more glorious work

of God than the creation of the whole materials universe (Harold Begbie, *Twice Born Men.* NY: Fleming H. Revell, 1909, p. 20)

The Salvation Army was about conversion, not about pledges of abstinence. And the Bible, in a verse often quoted by early AAs including old-timer Clarence Snyder, described the new creation as follows:

Therefore if any man be in Christ, he is a new creature: old things are passed away; behold, all things are become new (2 Corinthians 5:17).

Leslie D. Weatherhead was the scholar of the day who pointed out the psychologist's problem with the transformation. He wrote in speaking of guilt:

The lay psychologist seems to be helpless in such a situation. He tends to tell the patient that other people have done things just as bad, that he is making himself ill about nothing, that he must deflate his super-ego and get over his troubles as best he may. Religious treatment gets nearer to the heart of the matter, and if a real conversion takes place, the burden of guilt frequently disappears at once. But a conversion is not easily engineered. Further, a faulty theology, such as is only too common amongst us, because it is unacceptable to the intelligence of the twentieth century, fails adequately to deal with the situation. (Leslie D. Weatherhead, *Psychology, Religion and Healing.* NY: Abingdon-Cokesbury Press, 1951, p. 328)

All branches of the Christian Church agree that conversion is the way, from the religious side, to integration of personality. . . . Preaching aims at securing those conditions in which it happens. It is to be received. It cannot even be deserved or won. It is a gift of God in response to man's need and willingness by which God through Christ by His Spirit makes us one with Himself (Weatherhead, *supra*, p. 465).

In other words, the original Salvationist of Begbie's time was not dealing with guilt or pledges or decisions for abstinence. He was dealing with rescue. God had rescued the believer from the power of darkness and translated him into the kingdom of God's dear son. The believer was not counseled; was not adjured to turn away from selfish pursuits; and was not moved into rehab. On the streets, in the slums, of London, he was lovingly provided by the Salvationist with a living example of the deliverance and transformation that God's son had made possible—without therapy, lecture, or deed. He had only to accept the Saviour and, behold, would be changed.

Unfortunately, the Army itself seemed to yield to professionalism, and its people wrangled over the disease concept. Finally they adopted these two statements about 1940:

> "The Salvation Army believes that every individual who is addicted to alcohol may find deliverance from its bondage through submission of the total personality to the Lordship of Jesus Christ. The Salvation Army also recognizes the value of medical, social and psychiatric treatment for alcoholics and makes extensive use of these services at its centers." (White, *Slaying the Dragon, supra*, p. 78).

Note the compromised language. But let's take particular note of the description of the Salvation Army that was provided at the Yale Summer School of Alcohol Studies. Let's look in more detail at the lecture on Religious Bodies and Treatment of Inebriety, Rev. Francis W. McPeek said:

> Much work was done in city missions and particularly by the Salvation Army. The Army, however, has focused its efforts on the conversion experience and has made use of its own general facilities and of other community resources when these were needed in aftercare. Those who wish to read a portrayal of the Salvation Army's methods and approach may consult Hall's biography of Henry F. Milans (*Out of the Depth*). Generally speaking, the Salvationists have capitalized on the same techniques that have made other reform programs work: (1) Insistence on total abstinence; (2) reliance upon God; (3) the provision of new friendships among those who understand; (4) the opportunity to work with those who suffer from the same difficulty; and (5) unruffled patience and consistent faith in the ability of the individual and in the power of God to accomplish the desired ends. Francis W. McPeek, *Alcohol, Science and Society, Lecture 26, as given at the Yale Summer School of Alcohol Studies*. New Haven: Quarterly Journal of Studies on Alcohol, 1945, pp. 414-415.

Any reader who takes an honest look at McPeek's description of Salvation Army techniques of yesteryear and at the Frank Amos description of the early Akron program will see almost identical approaches. McPeek didn't talk about salvation, but the Army did. AAs didn't talk about salvation; they just took the newcomer upstairs and led him to accept Christ. In other words, abstinence, reliance upon the Creator, acceptance of Chirst, Christian fellowship, and Christian love and service worked for the Salvation Army, and it worked for the Akron Christian Fellowship.

C. The Keswick Colony of Mercy in Whiting, New Jersey. Founded in 1897 by William Raws who overcame alcoholism through religious salvation. Up to 39 men at a time reside there, undergoing Bible study, prayer, and counseling. They make a "pastoral covenant" to continued religious education and are expected to seek continued support through religious recovery groups such as Alcoholics Victorious. More than 17,000 alcoholic men have sought help there since its founding in 1897. (White, *Slaying the Dragon, supra*, pp. 75-76).

- **A Revival of Christian Healing through the person and power of Jesus Christ**

See Heal the Sick by James Moore Hickson (London: Methuen & Co., 1924). Hickson's book and extensive healing work were detailed in this title, which was one of the many healing books studied by Dr. Bob. It reports thousands of healings world-wide.

See Healing in Jesus Name by Ethel R. Willitts (Crawfordsville, Indiana: Ethel R. Willitts, Publisher, 1931). This review of Biblical healings and the personal healings by author Willits was studied by Dr. Bob.

See Psychology and Life by Leslie D. Weatherhead (New York: AbingdonPress,1935). Also, Leslie D. Weatherhead, Religion, Psychology and Healing, supra. Though Weatherhead's materials are heavy with writing on psychological, spiritualism, and psychic methods, Dr. Weatherhead was Minister of the City Temple in London and wrote exhaustively on the place of healing in the modern church. Highlighting the merits of Christian Science, he nonetheless rejects it, as he does the importance of healings at Lourdes. He then mentions the work of The Guild of Health, started in 1905 to arouse the Church of England and others to a fresh recognition of the place of health of mind and body in the Christian message. Next comes his discussion of The Guild of St. Raphael, formed in 1915, to push the Anglican Church and unite within the Catholic Church those who hold the faith that "Our Lord wills to work in and through His Church for the health of her members in spirit, mind, and body. Holy Unction, The Laying on of Hands, and intercessory prayer are utilized. Next, the Emmanuel Movement in America and the role of Worcester, Mc Comb, and Coriat. Next, Milton Abbey, opened in 1937 with Rev. John Maillard, an Anglican Clergyman as first warden–Maillard's book, *Healing in the Name of Jesus*, having just been published. Weatherhead next discusses The Divine Healing Mission, closely linked with the work of James Moore Hickson. He mentions The Friend's Spiritual Healing Fellowship (Quaker), The Methodist Society for Medical and Pastoral Practice, founded in 1946, The Churches' Council of Healing started in 1944 under the impetus of Archbishop Temple. Independently of the foregoing discussion of missions and individuals, Weatherhead analyzes the practice of intercession and The Laying on of Hands. And see the discussion of Weatherhead's materials in Dick B. *Dr. Bob and His Library* 3rd *ed.* (Kihei, HI: Paradise Research Publications, Inc., 1998), pp 78-79. There are many studies of the importance of the *charismata*, liturgies, anointing, sacraments, "unction," "incubation," shrines, demonology, exorcism, and the laying on of hands as part of Christian healing and Christian history. See Reverend F. W. Puller, *Anointing of the Sick: In Scripture and Tradition, With Some Considerations on the Numbering of the Sacraments, supra;* Dearmer, *Body and Soul, supra*, pp. 287 *et. seq.*; Evelyn Frost, *Christian Healing: A Consideration of the Place of Spiritual Healing in the Church of To-day in the Light of The Doctrine and Practice of the Ante-Nicene Church*, London: A. R. Mobray & Co. Limited, 1940; William Temple, *Christus Veritas An Essay* (London: Macmillan & Co Ltd, 1954); Dawson, *Healing: Pagan and Christian, supra;* Pridie, *The Church's Ministry of Healing, supra.*

And see the many other titles on healing and prayer that were studied and circulated by Dr. Bob among A.A. Pioneers and their families. See Dick B. *Dr. Bob and His Library, supra*, pp. 35-40, 83-85. In the early A.A. of Akron, there was circulation and study of a large number of prayer and healing books including those by Glenn

Clark, Starr Daily, Lewis L. Dunnington, Mary Baker Eddy, Charles and Cora Fillmore, Harry Emerson Fosdick, Emmet Fox, Gerald Heard, E. Stanley Jones, Frank Laubach, Charles Laymon, Rufus Mosely, William Parker, F. L. Rawson, Samuel M. Shoemaker, B. H. Streeter, L. W. Grensted, Howard Rose, Cecil Rose, St. Augustine, Brother Lawrence, Mary Tileston, Oswald Chambers, T. R. Glover, E. Herman, Donald Carruthers, and Nora Smith Holm with her *Runner's Bible.* See Dick B., *The Books Early AAs Read for Spiritual Growth*, 7th ed. (Kihei, HI: Paradise Research Publications, Inc., 1998). As our bibliography at the close of this book shows, and also as the foregoing citations as to healings make clear, the period of Dr. Bob's study of prayer and healing was one of widespread scholarly discourse on this very same subject. It does not seem surprising, therefore, that Dr. Bob observed prayer time at least three times a day; that he studied and quoted Scripture with great frequency; and that he was asked to and did in fact pray for others. As he himself expressed as to his beliefs: "Your Heavenly Father will never let you down!" (*Alcoholics Anonymous*, 4th ed., p. 181)

- **Successes of Oxford Group people in overcoming alcoholism prior to A.A.**

In their zeal to cut down the Oxford Group, many have ignored the well-documented victories over alcoholism through the power of God by well-known Oxford Group writers and leaders–most of whom were contemporaries or friends of Bill Wilson's. **These include Rowland Hazard, F. Shepard Cornell, Victor C. Kitchen, Ebby Thacher, James Houck, Charles Clapp, Jr., William Griffith Wilson, and even Russell Firestone and Richmond Walker for a time.** Both Dr. Frank N. D. Buchman (founder of the Oxford Group) and Rev. Samuel Shoemaker (its most prolific writer) helped sober up many drunks through the power of God. Their classic phrase was: Sin is the problem. Jesus Christ is the cure. The result is a miracle. See Dick B. *Cured!*, *supra*, pp. 18, 30-31.

The Present Tendency of Writers to Ignore our Real Spiritual Healing Roots and to Bloat up the Supposed Negative Lessons from of a Few, Unimportant, Unsuccessful, Little-known Predecessors at the turn of the Last Century

The Washingtonians. You can find more hoopla and writing among professionals, historians, and even AAs about the "Washingtonians" than you can about Dr. Bob, Anne Smith, Henrietta Seiberling, T. Henry Williams, and Rev. Sam Shoemaker–A.A.'s real founders. You can find more hoopla and writing by these same people about this same subject than you can about the Bible, Quiet Time, the Pioneers' devotionals, Sam Shoemaker's writings, other Christian literature, and Anne Smith's Journal–the major contributors to A.A. ideas. In a word or two, you need to recognize that the Washingtonians are a flash in the plan when it comes to their relevance to A.A. They were formed in 1840. They were deader than a door nail in 1847.

William White contends:

The Washingtonian Movement rose like a brilliant fireworks display on the American horizon, then it was all over. By 1845, the Washingtonian's energy was spent. What it had initiated could not be sustained. Almost none of the Washingtonian Societies were active beyond 1847 with the exception of those in Boston, which continued until the 1860's (White, *Slaying the Dragon*, *supra*, p. 12).

Then White nods to a real problem:

Contemporary church leaders of the period suggested that the Washingtonians failed because they ignored the crucial role of religion in the reformation of the alcoholic. While dissension on this point existed within the movement, most Washingtonians believed that social camaraderie was sufficient to sustain sobriety and that a religious component would only discourage drinkers from joining. . . . Some critics even went so far as to charge the Washingtonians with the heresy of humanism—elevating their own will above God's by failing to include religion in their meetings (White, *supra*, pp. 12-13).

If White's observations are accurate, they certainly repudiate much of the nonsense about the Washingtonians that you hear in A.A. today. We are told the Washingtonians give a good example of why A.A.'s Twelve Traditions were needed. We are told the Washingtonians flipped over because they were involved in "outside issues." But the simple fact is that they lacked the very elements which Akron A.A., the Salvation Army, and religious proponents of A.A. deem necessary. They lacked God! They lacked Jesus Christ! They lacked the Bible. And they lacked emphasis on prayer, God's guidance, and religious fellowship.

They did not offer the Bible, Quiet Time, the Creator, Jesus Christ, Christian literature, salvation, or religious principles that were the heart of A.A.'s spiritual program. So we will ignore them in this paper!

The Emmanuel Clinic and the Lay Therapy Movement. This was founded by two ministers and a physician in 1906. Its greatest problem is that it was a "psychological" approach to recovery. Worcester and Mc Comb said: "We do not plead for a return to the mere accidents of the early Christian age. . . . Great as is the power of the subconscious,, greater still, we believe, are the powers of reason, emotion, and will. Hence, one of the principal remedies for the nervous maladies of which we are speaking is psychic, moral, and religious re-education. . . . [we] say, 'God does it in and through the forces of nature.' The therapeutic procedures of the Emmanuel Movement are those which are used among all scientific workers, such as suggestion, psychic analysis, re-education, work, and rest" See Worcester and Mc Comb, *The Christian Religion as a Healing Power, supra,* pp. 96, 103, 118. Such talk probably burdened today's recovery community with many godless ideas about group therapy, individual counseling, self-help support, spirituality, hypnosis, relaxation, and "inspirational" reading. Its popular later book was *The Common Sense of Drinking* by Richard R. Peabody. And Peabody himself reportedly died intoxicated. It may well have fostered the "no cure" doctrine - once an alcoholic, always an alcoholic. And it can hardly said to be based on the power of God. So we will ignore this too.

The "Conversion" Solution that Dr. Carl Jung seems to have introduced into Bill Wilson's recovery thinking— the New York diversion that entered into Wilson's melting pot

Rowland Hazard's spiritual experience, better known as a religious conversion: According to Bill Wilson's early writings I found in Stepping Stones, at Bedford Hills, New York, A.A. really began when Rowland Hazard, once again drunk and despairing, returned to Dr. Carl Jung in Switzerland asking what he could do to whip his alcoholism. Jung replied: "Occasionally, Rowland, alcoholics have recovered through spiritual experiences, better known as religious conversions. . . . I'm talking about the kind of religious experience that reaches into the depths of a man, that changes his whole motivation and outlook and so transforms his life that the impossible becomes possible" (*W. G. Wilson, Reflections*, p. 111). Jung told Wilson many years later: "His [Rowland's] craving for alcohol was the equivalent on a low level of the spiritual thirst of our being for wholeness, expressed in medieval language: the union with God. . . . The only right and legitimate way to such an experience is, that it happens to you in reality and it can only happen when you walk on a path which leads to higher understanding" (Dick B., *Turning Point*, p. 84).

The unconvincing and unsupported claim that Rowland Hazard never visited with, or was told by Dr. Carl Jung that such a conversion was required for cure. Two writers have recently implied that the whole Rowland Hazard story and solution is a hoax (See White, *Slaying the Dragon*, *supra*, p.128). Their so-called "investigations" were scanty and lacking in comprehension and depth as they supposedly looked through Rowland's papers at the Rhode Island Historical Society and Jung's records and found no account of the doctor-patient event. To make this allegation stick, however, they would further have to prove that Rowland Hazard, Ebby Thacher, Bill Wilson, Rev. Sam Shoemaker, and Dr. Carl Jung were each and all outspoken liars. And, having "investigated" many of Rowland's records myself, and having been a trial attorney for many years with lots of experience in digging up evidence, and finding no reason to impeach the testimony of the foregoing accounts by Hazard, Thacher, Wilson, Shoemaker, and Jung, I believe the assertions of White and Wally P., the writers, who appear responsible for them, are totally wrong, scanty in depth, and a disservice to fact.

The peculiar and unique meaning of Jung's "conversion," "religious," and "spiritual" experience language. I personally have little doubt that Dr. Jung told Rowland Hazard that he (Jung) had been unsuccessful in treating, and could not cure Rowland. But what the Bible, theologians, and Christian evangelists mean by the prescribed "religious conversion" is probably not at all a conversion of the type to which Jung referred. First of all, Jung was a physician, not a cleric or theologian. Second, the Bible idea of conversion has to do with rebirth, of being born again of the spirit with the incorruptible seed of Christ, of confessing Jesus as Lord and believing that God raised Jesus from the dead (See John 3:1-17, 14:6; Acts 2:32-40, 4:10-12; Romans 10:9-10; Ephesians 1:12-14; Colossians 1:27; 1 Peter 1:18-23).

Dr. Leslie Weatherhead analyzed Jung's ideas as follows: "Jung seeks to lift the patient to a higher plane of living. What he calls "individualization" is an experience close to spiritual conversion. A true conception of both cannot regard either as final. Spiritual conversion is an experience which marks the end of man's search for the right road, but not the end of his spiritual journey. Individuation, in Jung's sense, is the wise setting of the house of one's personality in order, but it is a task at which one is wise to work for the rest of one's life" (Weatherhead, *Psychology, Religion and Healing, supra*, p. 287).

Jung himself said: "Religious experience is absolute. It is indisputable. You can only say that you never had such an experience, and your opponent will say: "Sorry, I have." And there your discussion will come to an end. No matter what the world thinks about religious experience, the one who has it possesses the great treasure of a thing that has provided him with a source of life, meaning and beauty and that has given a new splendor to the world and to mankind. He has pistis [believing or faith] and peace. Where is the criterium by which you could say that such a life is not legitimate, that such experience is not valid and that such *pistis* is a mere illusion? . . . But what is the difference between a real illusion and a healing religious experience? It is merely a difference in words (Jung, *Psychology and Religion*, pp. 113-114).

Jung's prescription for, and definition of, "religious" or "conversion" experience did not square with the Good Book. We can say: (1) Jung's definitions may be accurate from a psychologist's view point. In fact, they seem to be in agreement with the often quoted definitions of Professor William James. (2) But they are not speaking of being born from above with the incorruptible seed of Christ. (3) At Calvary Rescue Mission where Bill Wilson said he had been born again; and in Akron, where the A.A. pioneers accepted Jesus Christ as their Lord and Saviour, the folks were not quoting either Carl Jung or William James. They were quoting the Good Book. So was Rev. Sam Shoemaker. And so was Dr. Frank Buchman. (4) Hence, by turning back to William James and Carl Jung, Bill Wilson was led down the merry by-way to "spiritual" experience and "spiritual awakening"–both terms of Oxford Group manufacture–and later to just "personality change" sufficient to overcome alcoholism. (5) None of these has anything to do with what Jesus said was necessary in John 3:1-8 or with the conversation the Apostle Paul had with Jesus Christ on the Road to Damascus.

The Cures AA Pioneers Received Were Not Psychotherapeutic "Personality Changes." They Were Miracles. They were miracles produced by reliance on Yahweh, the Creator. And Both Bill Wilson and Dr. Bob Smith Were Very Clear in Attributing the Early A.A. Miracles to Their Heavenly Father, the Creator

Again, for the documentation, see Dick B. *Cured! Proven Help for Alcoholics and Addicts* (Kihei, HI: Paradise Research Publications, Inc., 2005); *When Early AAs Were Cured and Why* (Kihei, HI: Paradise Research Publications, Inc., 2006); Richard K. *New Freedom, supra.*

Now to the job of putting together the actual historical pieces of our pioneer A.A. program which relied for deliverance on the power of the Yahweh, the Creator–their God and mine.

4

The Spiritual Beginnings of A.A.

A.A.: Unique, But Borrowed

Bill Wilson often said: A.A. was not invented. He added: Each of A.A.'s spiritual principles was borrowed from ancient sources. Regrettably, Bill provided very very few specifics as to the actual sources of the spiritual principles, or just how they reached the A.A. fellowship.

Today, we can supply specific details. They have been gathered over a period of sixteen years from archives, interviews, historians, and the study of much literature. Those who did the A.A. borrowing and fashioning were A.A.'s founders, Bill W. and Dr. Bob. But one historical fact has been commonly lacking in discussions of the contributions of these two men. The Bill W. sources, spiritual infusions, and beliefs were totally different from those that came from Dr. Bob. Bill was a self-proclaimed "conservative atheist," had never belonged to a church, and had never studied the Bible until after he met Dr. Bob in Akron. Dr. Bob, on the other hand, had been a long-time Christian believer, church member, and Bible student since his youth. Regrettably, almost every A.A. historical account fails to take account of, earmark, and incorporate these differences and their A.A. impact.

Nonetheless, I sincerely hope you will leave this discussion with the impression that there were *not* two A.A. founding factions fighting with each other; *nor* were there two founders disagreeing with each other. **There were simply two distinctly different program origins**. And ultimately they produced two distinctly different results.

Two Distinctly Different Spiritual Origins

One of A.A.'s two origins might properly be called the "Carl Jung/Sam Shoemaker Source." It led to the "New York Genesis of A.A." Its ingredients are well-known and legendary, though inaccurately reported. Unfortunately, many incorrect aspects of the legend have become doctrinal.

A.A.'s other origin could properly be called the "Bible/Dr. Bob Source." It led to the "Akron Genesis of A.A." Unfortunately, the facts about this root remained virtually buried until our work began sixteen years ago.

The New York Genesis and its Dr. Carl Jung/Rev. Sam Shoemaker Source

We will dwell little on A.A.'s New York beginnings because they have so often been recorded, albeit mis-reported and distorted. To repeat: Bill Wilson, a Brooklyn resident, was a self-proclaimed "conservative atheist." He was never a church member, and had never "looked in the Bible at all" until he came to Akron in 1935 and met Dr. Bob.

The actual Bill Wilson picture as to A.A.'s "New York Genesis" and spiritual beginnings is as follows. An East Coast businessman named Rowland Hazard sought help for his alcoholism from Dr. Carl Jung in Switzerland. After his Jung treatment which was followed by relapse, Rowland was told by Jung that he had the mind of a chronic alcoholic and would need a conversion experience to overcome his compulsion. Jung defined such conversions as "union with God." He suggested Rowland seek a religious association.

Rowland therefore joined "A First Century Christian Fellowship" also known as the Oxford Group. Rowland followed its precepts; recovered from alcoholism; helped rescue a New Yorker named Ebby Thacher from alcoholism; taught Ebby the Oxford Group ideas; and later also spent substantial time with Bill Wilson inculcating Wilson with Oxford Group precepts.

Ebby Thacher visited and informed his suffering friend Bill Wilson that he (Ebby) had "got religion," that "God had done for him what he could not do for himself," and that he had been to Rev. Sam Shoemaker's Calvary Rescue Mission in New York.

A drunken Bill Wilson then went to Shoemaker's Rescue Mission, made a decision for Christ, believed he had really found something, and checked into Towns Hospital in New York. Bill had previously heard from his physician, Dr. William D. Silkworth, that there was a Great Physician (Jesus Christ) who could heal him. And, on his last trip to Towns, Bill heard some key Oxford Group principles during Ebby's visits to Bill at the hospital. In his own words, Bill had decided to call on the Great Physician for help. And this he did as he cried out: "If there be a God, let him show himself." Bill also then had what he often called his "hot flash" conversion experience. On release from Towns Hospital, Bill was totally unsuccessful: (1) In "converting" anyone to his Oxford Group ideas. (2) In getting one single drunk sober that Bill brought to the Wilson home for help. (3) For quite some time, in getting anyone sober in the New York area at all.

But Bill certainly assimilated some major Oxford Group life-changing principles–seemingly from the beginning of his sobriety in late 1934. These included the Five C's, the Four Absolutes, Surrender, Restitution, Guidance, Loyalty, Fellowship, and Witnessing. In all, these principles amounted to some twenty-eight Oxford Group ideas that were used to change lives and that impacted on Bill's idea that a "spiritual" or "conversion" experience could result from their practice. See Dick B. *The Oxford Group and Alcoholics Anonymous: A Design for Living That Works, 2d ed* (Kihei, HI: Paradise Research Publications, 1998). He endeavored to carry to drunks his version of that conversion message.

Not one recovered. Not during Bill's first six months of sobriety, nor for several years, in the case of those he and Lois took into their home. Very very few thereafter. In May, 1935, Bill carried his Oxford Group ideas to Dr. Bob in Akron, Ohio, where an entirely different chain of events had been in progress. See Dick B., *The Akron Genesis of Alcoholics Anonymous, 2d ed* (Kihei, HI: Paradise Research Publications, 1998).

The Akron Genesis and its Bible/Dr. Bob Source

A.A.'s Akron Genesis began with Dr. Bob, his church activities as a youngster, and his excellent Bible and religious training in the North Congregational Church at St. Johnsbury, Vermont, where he and his parents worshipped. Also in Bob's participation in the Christian Endeavor youth movement in churches in those days. See Dick B., *Dr. Bob and His Library*, 3rd ed. (Kihei, HI: Paradise Research Publications, Inc., 1998); *The James Club and The Original Program's Absolute Essentials*, 4th ed., *supra*.

Dr. Bob was born and raised in St. Johnsbury, Vermont. His parents were pillars of the North Congregational Church in St. Johnsbury. From childhood through high school, Bob each week attended that Congregational church, its Sunday School, evening service, Monday night Christian Endeavor meetings, and sometimes its Wednesday evening prayer meeting. These actions were likely at the insistence of his mother. Yet, Bob continued membership in Christian churches most of his life: St. Johnsbury Congregational in his youth. Possibly St. Luke's Protestant Episcopal Church. Probably the Church of Our Saviour in Akron, where his kids attended Sunday School. Then Akron's Westminster Presbyterian Church where Dr. Bob and his wife Anne Smith were charter members from June 3, 1936 to April 3, 1942. Finally, a year before his death, Dr. Bob became a communicant at St. Paul's Episcopal Church in Akron. This Episcopal Church was the so-called "Firestone" church of which Dr. Walter Tunks was rector and who had so much to do with A.A.'s Akron beginnings.

Dr. Bob specifically told AAs he had nothing to do with writing the Twelve Steps. Nor did he have much to do with the writing of A.A.'s basic text, the "Big Book," other than to review manuscripts as Bill Wilson passed them to Bob for approval prior to publication in the Spring of 1939. But Dr. Bob did make some very clear statements about the Bible and A.A. And it was from and in Akron that A.A.'s basic biblical ideas were discussed, honed, tried, and then later put into terse and tangible form at Bill Wilson's hands in A.A.'s "Big Book" and Twelve Steps.

Dr. Bob said A.A.'s basic ideas came from the Bible. Both Dr. Bob and Bill often stated that Jesus's sermon on the mount contained the underlying spiritual philosophy of A.A. Bob often read Bible passages from the sermon (which is found in Matthew Chapters Five, Six, and Seven). Bob specifically pointed out that the A.A. slogans "First Things First" and "Easy Does It" were taken respectively from Matthew 6:33 and 6:34. Furthermore, when someone asked Dr. Bob a question about the A.A. program, his usual response was: "What does it say in the Good Book?" He declared that A.A. pioneers were "convinced that the answer to their problems was in the Good Book." He added: "To some of us older ones, the parts we found absolutely essential were the Sermon on the Mount, the 13th chapter of First Corinthians, and the Book of James." In fact, James was so popular with the pioneers that, according to Bill Wilson, many favored calling the A.A. fellowship "The James Club."

The Biblical emphasis in A.A.'s "Akron Group No. One" involved much much more. The pioneer meetings opened with Christian prayer. The leader always had an open Bible in front of him. As mentioned, the weekly meetings were "old fashioned prayer meetings." Bible devotionals such as *The Upper Room*, *My Utmost for His Highest*, and *The Runner's Bible* were regular fare. Also in individual Quiet Times, and Quiet Times with Anne Smith each morning at the Smith home. Quiet Time itself had very clear Biblical roots. See Dick B., *Good Morning!: Quiet Time, Morning Watch, Meditation, and Early A.A.*, 2d ed. (Kihei, HI: Paradise Research Publications, Inc., 1998). Scripture was regularly read at all meetings. Scripture, both from devotionals and from actual reading of the Good Book, was often the fountainhead for topics discussed at pioneer meetings. Bible study itself was stressed. Dr. Bob called every meeting of early A.A. a "Christian Fellowship;" and early A.A. was in fact an integral part of "A First Century Christian Fellowship." Also, as will be detailed later, every single Twelve Step idea can be traced to specific Bible verses and segments. Furthermore, "Surrenders" were required in early Akron A.A. These meant accepting on one's knees Jesus Christ as Lord and Saviour. Older members then prayed with newcomers in the manner specified in James 5:16. See Dick B., *The Good Book and The Big Book: A.A.'s Roots in the Bible*, 2d ed. (Kihei, HI: Paradise Research Publications, Inc., 1997); *The Akron Genesis of Alcoholics Anonymous*, supra; *DR. BOB and the Good Oldtimers*, supra; *That Amazing Grace: The Role of Clarence and Grace S. in Alcoholics Anonymous* (Kihei, HI: Paradise Research Publications, Inc., 1986).

And how did all these Christian and Bible-oriented principles and practices find their way into the early Akron program? Certainly not from, nor properly described as through, Bill Wilson. They were the daily grist of the Akron experimental work to deliver drunks. Program ideas with which Dr. Bob had been familiar since his Vermont days.

The Christian Endeavor Society Impact

That introduces a final point. One that really marks the beginning of the Akron Genesis. Its details were only recently unearthed in the author's research. It has to do with Christian Endeavor, the Christian church movement for youth to which Dr. Bob belonged as a youngster. And that movement, its practices, and principles can be seen as having great impact on many of the basic and unique aspects of Akron A.A.. These aspects differed from the Oxford Group approaches and principles with which Bill Wilson had been indoctrinated on the East Coast. They did not involve the Four Absolutes, nor the 5 C's, nor Restitution, nor Guidance as such, nor the Surrenders, nor the house-parties, nor the teams, nor other distinctly Oxford Group ideas with which Bob and Bill were both familiar from their respective Oxford Group connections.

Akron Christian Endeavor Resemblances: Akron A.A.'s prayer meetings, Bible study, devotional literature, religious discussions, confession of Christ, emphasis on church affiliation, and Christian outreach were a distinct characteristic of the Akron program. They were not emphasized in New York. They showed the influence that Christian Endeavor had on Dr. Bob. See Dick B., *The Books Early AAs Read for Spiritual Growth,* 7th ed. (Kihei, HI: Paradise Research Publications, 1998, pp. 13-17); *Cured!: Proven Help for Alcoholics and Addicts* (Kihei, HI: Paradise Research Publications, Inc., 2003); *Dr. Bob and His Library,* 3rd ed. (Kihei, HI: Paradise Research Publications, Inc., 1998); Amos R. Wells, *Expert Endeavor: A Textbok of Christian Endeavor Methods and Principles* (Boston: United Society of Christian Endeavor, 1911); Francis E. Clark. *Christian Endeavor in All Lands.* (N.p.: The United Society of Christian Endeavor, 1906); *Memoirs of Many Men in Many Lands: An*

Autobiography (Boston: United Society of Christian Endeavor, 1922); James DeForest Murch, *Successful C.E. Prayer-Meetings* (Cincinnati: The Standard Publishing Company, 1930).

The Christian Endeavor Movement: Christian Endeavor was a movement formed in Williston Congregational Church in Portland, Maine on February 2, 1881. It was designed to meet the need of the church for training young Christians. Activities included the weekly young people's prayer meeting. Each member promised to attend and take some part. A Bible verse or a sentence of prayer answered the individual's obligation of "taking some part aside from singing." In addition to prayer meetings, there were social gatherings, missionary committees, music and floral committees, and committees to visit the sick and poor and welcome strangers. The organization endeavored, like its offspring Akron A.A., to be self-governing and self-propagating. It spread to Massachusetts, Rhode Island, and Vermont. Then to numerous U.S. churches, to Hawaii, China, and many parts of the world. In a few years, nearly 25,000 young people journeyed across the United States to attend a convention in San Francisco.

Principles and Practices: Rev. Francis E. Clark, Founder of the Christian Endeavor Movement, said the roots of the Christian Endeavor tree were: (1) Confession of Christ. (2) Service for Christ. (3) Fellowship with Christ's people. (4) And Loyalty to Christ's Church. As to the Confession of Christ, Clark said: "Confession of Christ is absolutely necessary in the Christian Endeavor Society. . . . Every week comes the prayer meeting in which every member who fulfills his vow must take some part. . . . The true Christian Endeavorer. . . .does take part to show that he is a Christian, to confess his love for the Lord. . . . The covenant pledge. . . secures familiarity with the Word of God by promoting Bible-reading and study in preparation for every meeting.

Rev. F. B. Meyer, who later was to have a substantial influence on the Oxford Group and on early A.A. ideas and was president of the British Christian Endeavor Union, said Christian Endeavor stood for five great principles: (1) Personal devotion to the divine Lord and Saviour, Jesus Christ. (2) The covenant obligation embodied in our pledge. (3) Constant religious training for all kinds of service. (4) Strenuous loyalty to the local church and denomination with which each society is connected. (5) Interdenominational spiritual fellowship.

The C.E. founder, Rev. Francis Clark, summarized the C.E. covenant as follows: "Trusting in the Lord Jesus for strength, I promise him that I will strive to do whatever He would like to have me do; that I will pray and read the Bible every day; and that, just so far as I know how, I will endeavor to lead a Christian life. I will be present at every meeting of the society, unless prevented by some reason which I can conscientiously give to my Saviour, and will take part in the meeting, either by prayer, testimony, or a Bible verse. As an active member of this society, I promise to be faithful to my own church, and to do all I can to uphold its works and membership."

Amos R. Wells, Editorial Secretary of the United Society of Christian Endeavor, asked: (1) What are the results we may gain from the prayer meeting? They are five: original thought on religious subjects; open committal to the cause of Christ; the helpful expression of Christian thought and experience; the cultivation of the spirit of worship through public prayer and singing; the guidance of others along these lines of service and life. (2) How can we get original thought on the prayer-meeting topics? Only by study of the Bible, followed by meditation. First, the Endeavorer should read the Bible passage; then he should read some good commentary upon it; then he should take the subject with him into his daily life. (3) Are we to read Bible verses and other quotations? Yes, all we please, if we will make them the original expression of our own lives by thinking about them, and adding to them something, if only a sentence, to show that we have made them our own. If you read A.A.'s *DR. BOB and the Good Oldtimers*, as well as my own titles on early A.A., you will see unique Christian Endeavor parallels and practices in what was called the Akron "Program." In fact, if you read the personal stories of the pioneers in the First Edition of A.A.'s Big Book, you will see the practices in action.

To be sure, the Akron pioneers sometimes called themselves the alcoholic squad of the Oxford Group (*DR. BOB and the Good Oldtimers, supra,* p. 117). They also called themselves a "Christian fellowship" (*DR. BOB, supra,* p. 118) as well as the "Alcoholic Group of Akron, Ohio" (*DR. BOB, supra,* p. 128). But their unique meeting structure was not like that of most Oxford Group meetings or "house parties." In fact, they were also called a "clandestine" or secret lodge of that Group (*DR. BOB*, *supra*, p. 121). Moreover, the Akron practices were not familiar to eastern Oxford Grouper Bill Wilson when he came to Akron. This, in part, because Akron meetings resembled Christian Endeavor meetings in a number of ways—ways that clearly unfamiliar to New Yorker Wilson: As stated, the Akron A.A. meetings were called "old fashioned prayer meetings" and "Christian Fellowships." Group study of the Bible, meditation. reading of Bible literature, and discussion of topics from the Bible as they impacted on the member's life all contained ingredients different from those at Sam Shoemaker's Calvary House in New York—the place where Bill Wilson received most, albeit little, of the Oxford Group instruction in his early days.

So too Akron's mandatory surrender to Jesus Christ, self-support and self-propagation credo, emphasis on alignment with some church, fellowship with like-minded believers, service, and witness.

These Akron elements caused it to be described as first century Christianity such as that found in the Book of Acts (*DR. BOB*, *supra*, pp.129-31, 135-36); and these elements were the heart of Akron A.A.

Most assuredly, common spillovers from Oxford Group life-changing techniques were also present in both New York and Akron A.A. beginnings. But the Akron Genesis was unquestionably biblical.

Melding the Roots was solely a Bill Wilson Project

After a nose count of the early successes in 1937, and in the midst of substantial controversy, Bill Wilson obtained a split vote in Akron that authorized him to write a basic text describing the practices and program pioneer AAs had developed to achieve their astonishing successes, which were said to be seventy-five percent.

But Bill did not do the expected. In fashioning the basic text, Bill took some simple medical facts about alcoholism and the alcoholic that he had learned from his own physician Dr. William D. Silkworth. He added substantial practical treatment ideas, probably from Richard R.

Peabody's book, *The Common Sense of Drinking* (Atlantic Monthly Press Book, 1933). He mentioned neither the Bible nor Jesus Christ in connection with his reported program, but he adopted much from the Akron surrenders. From the Oxford Group, Wilson codified in A.A. the Oxford Group life-changing techniques (Surrenders, the 5 C's, the Four Absolutes, Guidance, and Restitution). To this mix, he added (using Oxford Group terms like spiritual experience and later spiritual awakening) his own "religious" experience, calling them all the process of finding God. See *Alcoholics Anonymous*, 1st ed., 1939. And this concept of "finding God" was one about which Rev. Sam Shoemaker had been writing since his first significant book in 1923—*Realizing Religion*. Unfortunately, Bill left to others, if to anyone at all, the unearthing of source details. The digging–certainly mine–goes on to this day. See: Dick B., *Dr. Bob and His Library*; *Good Morning: Quiet Time, Morning Watch, Meditation and Early A.A.*; *The Good Book and The Big Book*; *The Akron Genesis of Alcoholics Anonymous*; *New Light on Alcoholism*; *Turning Point*; *The Oxford Group and Alcoholics Anonymous*; and Bill Pittman and Dick B., *Courage to Change The Christian Roots of the Twelve-Step Movement*.

Dick B.'s web sites on the early A.A. history are
http://www.dickb.com/index.shtml; http://www.dickb-blog.com; http://aa-history.com; http://freedomranchmaui.org.

5

The Real Program of Early A.A.

At The First Nationwide Alcoholics Anonymous History Conference in Phoenix, I said the following as to this section: "We want to cover three features of the actual program before we hear from Smitty (Dr. Bob's son) about living with his Dad: (1) A brief overview of exactly what the pioneers did as they fashioned their program in Akron between June 10, 1935 and the publication of the Big Book in the Spring of 1939. (2) A summary by Frank Amos of the results of his thorough investigation of the Akron successes, his report to John D. Rockefeller, Jr., and what that actual program was. (3) A synopsis of the seven basic Biblical sources of that program." See Dick B., *The First Nationwide Alcoholics Anonymous History Conference, 2d ed.*, Kihei, HI: Paradise Research Publications, Inc., 2006)

An Overview of What They Did in Akron

Hospitalization for about seven days: Only a Bible in the room, medications, daily visits and lengthy talks by Dr. Bob, visits by recovered pioneers, belief in God, surrender to Christ, and prayer. Then discharge from the hospital.

Recovery in the homes: (1) Daily get-togethers, (2) Bible study and reading, (3) Individual quiet times, (4) Quiet Times in the morning with Anne Smith, (5) discussions with Bob and Henrietta and Anne, (6) the regular Wednesday meeting, with "real" surrenders upstairs (James 5:15-16: Elders and prayer), acceptance of Jesus Christ, asking God to take alcohol out of their lives, and asking Him to help them abide by the Four Absolutes. (7) Some individual Oxford Group elements such as Inventory, Confession, Conviction, and Restitution. (8) Visiting newcomers at the hospital. (9) Church attendance by most. (9) Social, religious, and family fellowship.

Regular Wednesday Meetings: Prayer, Scripture, Group Prayer and Guidance, Discussion, Surrender, appeal for helping newcomers, Lord's Prayer, socializing, and exchange of literature. No drunkalogs. No steps. No Big Book. Just the Bible which they affectionately called the "Good Book" and devotionals like the *Upper Room.* Dr. Bob's son described the meetings as "old fashioned revival meetings." And they bore much resemblance to the Bible study, prayer, conversion, Quiet Hour activities of the United Christian Endeavor Society of Dr. Bob's youth.

Quiet Time (with Anne, with Group, or individual): Based first on having accepted Jesus Christ; there was Bible reading; prayer and seeking guidance; use of devotionals; use of *Anne Smith's Journal*; reading of Christian literature.

Working with newcomers: The greatest dearth in today's recovery work is the absence of Twelfth Stepping—working with newcomers. Yet this focus on finding and helping still-suffering alcoholics was unquestionably the primary unique factor of early A.A. Although it resembled Christian witnessing, it was perhaps the main unusual feature of A.A. itself in that it focused only on alcoholics and, in the beginning, largely on the hospitalization phase. It's something Wilson did from the very start of his sobriety. See *Pass It On.* It's something that Akron did from the get-go. See Dick B., *Henrietta Seiberling: Ohio's Lady with a Cause;* and *The Akron Genesis of Alcoholics Anonymous.* It's something that Bill and Bob and the pioneers did constantly. It's something for which Clarence Snyder became a crackerjack, tireless outreach man in Cleveland. See Mitch K., *How It Worked.* And it's something that Dr. Bob and Sister Ignatia did with some 5000 alcoholics at St. Thomas Hospital. See Mary Darrah, *Sister Ignatia: Angel of Alcoholics Anonymous.*

Confirmation by Bill and Bob together in 1943: The statements of Bill and Bob together at the Shrine Auditorium in Los Angeles in 1943 are most informative. There were some 4500 present. Bill spoke about Divine Aid, the religious element, and prayer. Dr. Bob spoke about cultivating the habit of prayer and reading the Bible. Both men were warmly received.

The Frank Amos Reports in 1938

John D. Rockefeller, Jr. had been asked to fund the fledgling A.A. He had received glowing accounts from Bill Wilson of the great successes in the Akron program being led by Dr. Bob.

Rockefeller wanted to learn for himself. He sent his agent Frank Amos to investigate the Akron scene; and Amos did a thorough job. He interviewed founders, A.A. members, relatives, judges, physicians, and others. And his remarks included the following:

> "All considered practically incurable by physicians." They had "been reformed and so far have remained teetotalers." Stories were remarkably alike in "the technique used and the system followed."

Mr. Amos described their seven-point "Program" as follows:

[**Abstinence**] An alcoholic must realize that he is an alcoholic, incurable from a medical viewpoint, and that he must never again drink anything with alcohol in it.

[**Absolute reliance on the Creator**] He must surrender himself absolutely to God, realizing that in himself there is no hope.

[**Removal of sins from his life**] Not only must he want to stop drinking permanently, he must remove from his life other sins such as hatred, adultery, and others which frequently accompany alcoholism. Unless he will do this absolutely, Smith and his associates refuse to work with him.

[**Daily Quiet Time with Bible study and prayer**] He must have devotions every morning–a "quiet time" of prayer and some reading from the Bible and other religious literature. Unless this is faithfully followed, there is grave danger of backsliding.

[**Helping other alcoholics**] He must be willing to help other alcoholics get straightened out. This throws up a protective barrier and strengthens his own willpower and convictions.

[**Fellowship**] It is important, but not vital, that he meet frequently with other reformed alcoholics and form both a social and a religious comradeship.

[**Religious affiliation**] Important, but not vital, that he attend some religious service at least once weekly.

See Dick B. *God and Alcoholism: Our Growing Opportunity in the 21st Century* (Kihei, HI: Paradise Research Publications, Inc., 2002); *DR. BOB and the Good Oldtimers, supra,* p. 131.

The Major Biblical Roots of the Original Program

Dr. Bob said quite plainly that A.A."s basic ideas came from the Bible. His words were echoed by his venerable sponsee Clarence Snyder. Bill said the Steps came primarily from the Oxford Group principles as taught by Reverend Sam Shoemaker of New York. Nonetheless, Shoemaker himself had been described as a "Bible Christian"—whose sermons and writings were filled with Biblical references. See Irving Harris, *The Breeze of the Spirit.* As stated, there were not two competing programs. There were simply two different founders, coming from two totally different backgrounds, and receiving their initial recovery ideas from two totally different sources.

The Oxford Group said plainly that its principles were the principles of the Bible. Both Dr. Bob and Bill said that Jesus's sermon on the mount (Matthew 5, 6, 7) contained the underlying A.A. philosophy. And from this beginning picture, my sixteen years of research led me to believe that the following seven major spiritual roots of Alcoholics Anonymous are Biblical in origin and form. These are the seven:

The Bible. See Dick B., ***The Good Book and The Big Book: A.A.'s Roots in the Bible.*** Over and over the Bible was stressed as the basic source of our ideas: The focus of reading was the Sermon on the Mount, 1 Corinthians 13, and the Book of James. But, as outlined hereafter, there were many other Bible verses that were commonly applied. See the detailed review of the three segments and of the other verses in Dick B., *Why Early A.A. Succeeded* (Kihei, HI: Paradise Research Publications, Inc., 2001); *The James Club and the Original*

A.A. Program's Absolute Essentials. In addition, plenty was taught, studied, and taken from the Ten Commandments, Psalms, Proverbs, Acts, Jesus's Two Great Commandments, the need for a new birth by receiving from above God's spirit in Christ, prayer, healing, repentance, guidance, forgiveness, and so on. See also Dick B., *The Akron Genesis of Alcoholics Anonymous, supra; Anne Smith's Journal, 1933-1939,* 3rd ed. Kihei, HI: Paradise Research Publications, Inc., 1998.

Quiet Time. The born-again newcomer was to grow in knowledge, principles, and practices from the Bible. He was to study the Bible. He was to cultivate the habit of prayer. He was to give thanks and to forgive. He was to observe a quiet period for doing these things. And, in the Oxford Group, the practice was called first "The Morning Watch" and later "Quiet Time. In Christian Endeavor, it was called "Quiet Hour;" and it was considered so important that observing members were called "Comrades of the Quiet Hour." Often, in the A.A. meetings and fellowships in they morning, there were discussions of Bible topics, just as people at done in the United Christian Endeavor Society of Dr. Bob's early days. Furthermore, the members were to seek guidance from Yahweh, the Creator. They were advised to read religious books and use daily devotionals. This was done individually, with Dr. Bob's wife, Anne, and at meetings. See Dick B., *Good Morning!, supra; Anne Smith's Journal, 1933-1939, supra.*

Anne Smith's Journal. This remarkable account by Dr. Bob's wife is the most-forgotten and ignored source of A.A. ideas. Anne says it all. She was "it" as far as recording the real early A.A. program ideas in detail. She wrote them down in organized fashion in 64 pages from 1933 to 1939. And she shared abundantly from that journal with AAs and their families. There is every reason to believe that Bill's Oxford Group language in the Big Book was derived from what he heard and read with Anne Smith in Akron in the summer of 1935. See Dick B., *Anne Smith's Journal, 1933-1939, supra.*

The Teachings of Reverend Sam Shoemaker. Bill attributed practically all the Steps and ideas to Sam and called him a co-founder of A.A. Bill even asked Sam to write the Twelve Steps, though Sam declined and told Bill that they should be written by an alcoholic, namely Bill. Sam reviewed Bill's first Big Book manuscripts before they were published. And Sam's words, language, and ideas can be found in the Steps and in the Big Book. See Dick B., *New Light on Alcoholism: God, Sam Shoemaker, and A.A.*, 2d ed. (Kihei, HI: Paradise Research Publications, Inc., 1999); *Twelve Steps for You: Take the Steps with the Big Book, A.A. History, and the Bible at Your Side*, 3rd ed. Kihei, HI: Paradise Research Publications, Inc., 2006.

The life-changing program of the Oxford Group. No matter how hard he tried to distance himself and AA from the Oxford Group, the simple fact is that Bill's whole Big Book program is Oxford Group in character, principles, and practices. That fact was made quite clear in A.A.'s own biography of Wilson, *Pass It On*. NY: Alcoholics Anonymous World Services, Inc., 1984. Bill worked closely with Sam Shoemaker. While Dr. Bob really had little to do with Shoemaker, he and Anne, Henrietta, and the Williams couple were thorough readers of Oxford Group literature and were thoroughly conversant with its ideas. See Dick B., *The Oxford Group and Alcoholics Anonymous, supra; By the Power of God, supra; Twelve Steps for You, supra; Henrietta Seiberling: Ohio's Lady with a Cause.*

The books early AAs read for spiritual growth. The pioneers in Akron were readers. They were spurred on by Dr. Bob, Anne, and Henrietta. They read the Bible. They read the devotionals - *The Runner's Bible, The Upper Room, My Utmost for His Highest*. They read commentaries like *As a Man Thinketh, The Greatest Thing in the World*, Fox's *The Sermon on the Mount*, and books by the great religious leaders and writers - Glenn Clark, E. Stanley Jones, Oswald Chambers, Harry Emerson Fosdick, Norman Vincent Peale, Henry Drummond, and many many others. They read the Shoemaker books and the Oxford Group books, of which there were more than 500 in all. See Dick B. *Making Known the Biblical History and Roots of Early Alcoholics Anonymous, 3rd ed.* Kihei, HI: Paradise Research Publications, Inc., 2006. You could see references to these writings in the *Cleveland Central Bulletin*, in the *AA Grapevine*, and in the Akron AA pamphlets. See Dick B., *The Books Early AAs Read for Spiritual Growth*, 7th ed., *supra*; *Dr. Bob and His Library*, 3rd ed., *supra*; and *Making Known the Biblical Roots of Early A.A., supra*

The principles and practices of the United Christian Endeavor Society. Today, after reading an immense amount of Christian

Endeavor literature, after absorbing what they did in their meetings with conversions, Bible study, prayer, Quiet Hour, specifically stressing love, and service, I am convinced that their procedure was the one that heavily impacted upon and perhaps even was codified by Dr, Bob ultimately in the Akron Christian Fellowship program he led. I believe that is one of the several reasons that Dr. Bob specifically described all the meetings as Christian and the alcoholic squad as a Christian Fellowship. See Dick B. *The James Club, supra; God and Alcoholism, supra.*

Other sources that certainly filtered into Bill Wilson's Big Book and into the reading by Akronites were, though unusual in content and character, from New Thought writers like Ralph Waldo Emerson, Phineas P. Quimby, Mary Baker Eddy, Ralph Waldo Trine, James Allen, Emmet Fox, Charles Fillmore, Horatio W. Dresser, F. L. Rawson, Thomas Troward, and William James. And almost all of these quoted Scripture at some length. See Dick B., *Cured!, supra; God and Alcoholism, supra,* pp. 77-118; and *Making Known the Biblical Roots of A.A., supra.* A.A. historian Mel B., himself a New Thought adherent and also an AA with some 54 years of sobriety, wrote:

> The spiritual program of A.A. also has elements of transcendentalism and existentialism, though not as a result of any conscious studies of these philosophies by Bill (Mel B., *My Search for Bill W.* Center City, MN: Hazelden, 2000, p. 4)

I would add the comment that, while Bill may or may not have studied "these philosophies," he was certainly exposed to mountains of mysticism through his own extensive interest in spiritualism and through the Swendenborgian background in the life of his wife, Lois. "Cosmic consciousness," "fourth dimension," and "higher power" language do not seem to have been part of the Akron pioneer diet.

6

The Materials from the Bible That Dr. Bob Considered "Absolutely Essential"

Introductory Comments

Jesus's Sermon on the Mount (Matthew 5-7), the Book of James, and 1 Corinthians 13 were specified over and over by Dr. Bob as absolutely essential to the early program in Akron.

But Dr. Bob painted with wide brush strokes when it came to the Bible as a whole. Note the following newspaper article:

> "Dr. Bob, another founder of A.A., also addressed the Shrine assembly [along with Bill W.] As he was introduced, the audience rose to its feet in tribute. The fame of Dr. Bob is great in A.A. In soft, confident and unhurried words he too [along with Bill W.] reiterated the principles of Alcoholics Anonymous. . . He particularly recommended reading the Bible" (*The Tidings*, Friday, March 26, 1943, p. 47).

The Bible Was King in the Early Program. You met and used it at every turn.

Some would like to employ Bill's regrettable remark about "fear of being God-bitten" and imply that the A.A. pioneers were out on street corners and standing on soap boxes thumping the Word. But that was not the case at all. The Bible was ever-present in the fellowship itself, but the pioneers were listeners not preachers. They were students not teachers. They were readers not writers. Dr. Bob, Anne, Henrietta

Seiberling, and T. Henry Williams and his wife saw to it that the early A.A. Christian Fellowship members were fed the milk of the Word in every possible way but in moderate spoon fulls. And the reason was quite simple: The pioneers were not well-versed in the very truths which were needed to get them well.

The Picture of the Bible's Use

Basic Resource: My most comprehensive work on A.A.'s Bible roots is *The Good Book and The Big Book: A.A.'s Roots in the Bible.* It seems to have been the most popular of my twenty-six published titles; and it has been the most frequently purchased. This fundamental book gives you the broad picture of just which basic ideas AAs took from the Bible; and I'll mention the principal ones in a moment.

The Akron Founders: But you encounter the Bible in any honest, careful research of A.A. history—whether of the early years or some of the later years. Dr. Bob's own Bible study heads the list, and he received excellent training in it as a youngster. It was a paramount study in the United Christian Endeavor Society in which Dr. Bob was so active as a youth, and he continued to read and study it from cover to cover throughout his life, but particularly when he got sober. His wife, Anne Smith, was equally well versed in the Bible and actually read it to Bill and Bob daily in the formative summer of 1935. Then she read it daily as part of the Quiet Times she held each morning at the Smith home, and she frequently quotes and discusses it in the journal she kept and shared with AAs and their families. See Dick B., *Anne Smith's Journal, supra.* I have personally seen Henrietta Seiberling's Bible and the extensive notes and leaflets she used. Her children confirmed her devotion to it. See Dick B., *Henrietta Seiberling: Ohio's Lady with a Cause, supra.* T. Henry and Clarace Williams were Bible students from the get-go. T. Henry had taught Sunday School and Clarace had studied to be a missionary. See Dick B., *The Akron Genesis, supra.* These people therefore provided a phalanx of Bible teachers in early A.A.

The Oxford Group and Shoemaker A.A.'s connection with the Oxford Group has been discussed at length elsewhere. See Dick B., *The Oxford Group and Alcoholics Anonymous* and *New Light on*

Alcoholism, supra. And it is quite clear that: (1) Dr. Frank N.D. Buchman, Oxford Group founder, was "soaked in the Bible," as one writer stated and that he insisted that Oxford Group people in New York receive Bible instruction from a Miss Mary Angevine who was skilled in that subject. (2) Rev. Samuel M. Shoemaker, Jr., an American Leader of the Oxford Group, was known as a "Bible Christian." He filled his books, articles, sermons, and radio talks with Bible verses and ideas. See Irving Harris, *The Breeze of the Spirit.* (3) I don't think I've read a single Oxford Group book that hasn't talked a great deal about the Bible. See Dick B., *Making Known the Biblical History and Roots of Alcoholics Anonymous, supra.*

The Daily Devotionals: AAs regularly observed Quiet Time and used devotionals in connection with it. The Bible was always read. And each of the favored devotionals featured Bible verses and study. They certainly included *The Upper Room, The Runner's Bible*, E. Stanley Jones' *Victorious Living*, Fosdick's *The Meaning of Prayer*, Tileston's *Daily Strength for Daily Needs*, and *My Utmost for His Highest*. See Dick B. *Good Morning: Quiet Time, Morning Watch, Meditation, and Early A.A.* Most of these specific devotionals are still widely read, have often been reprinted, and can be found in Christian outlets today.

The Biblical subjects in the many Christian Books Dr. Bob and Anne read and circulated Almost every book that was recommended to, and circulated among, the early AAs by Dr. Bob personally and by Anne Smith was a Bible-related book. Thus Drummond's *The Greatest Thing in the World*, Emmet Fox's *The Sermon on the Mount*, Glenn Clark's *The Soul's Sincere Desire*, E. Stanley Jones' *The Christ of the Mount*, Toyohiko Kagawa's *Love: The Law of Life*; and the many many books by Harry Emerson Fosdick fit the category of Bible-related. For the whole picture and for other Bible-related literature they read, see Dick B., *Dr. Bob and His Library*, 3rd ed; *The Books Early AAs Read for Spiritual Growth*, 7th ed;, *That Amazing Grace; Making Known the Biblical History and Roots, supra.* Recently, one mid-west A.A. historian found a list published in 1940 and naming some 10 books that were allegedly the reading fare of the pioneers. But his hypothesis is far from based on the facts. I personally have seen the books in Dr. Bob's Library—dozens of them. I personally have seen copies of Anne Smith's Journal in which Anne recommended all kinds of books other than those the scholar mentioned. I personally have collected and read almost all of the more than 500 Oxford Group and Shoemaker titles that were available in the early years. And all attest to the erroneous view that somehow early A.A. reading was confined to a list of 10 New Thought books. A brief visit to the Griffith Library at Bill Wilson's birthplace, or to the Shoemaker collection at Calvary Church in Pittsburgh, or to Dr. Bob's Home in Akron would dispel this myth. There are hundreds of early A.A. books available for all to see and read.

Many of the Bible's Books, Parts, and Verses Need Specific Mention Here.

A.A.'s Bible roots are as numerous and varied as the A.A. sources that used them. If you start with the Bible *devotionals* in wide use by A.A.'s old-timers, you'll see lots of mention of *all* the Bible verses, chapters, and books we'll discuss in the various parts of this presentation. Key among the devotionals were *The Upper Room, The Runner's Bible, Daily Strength for Daily Needs,* and *My Utmost For His Highest.* These books and pamphlets covered many verses and segments of the Bible other than the Sermon on the Mount, the Book of James, and 1 Corinthians 13. Many of these other verses and segments were studied by, and important to, A.A.'s pioneers. You can find them mentioned almost anywhere you start.

If you start with the books Dr. Bob's wife Anne recommended and shared from her journal with early AAs and their families, you will find Anne recommending the Book of Acts, Psalms, Proverbs, the Gospels, and other specific sections. She also recommended Fosdick's book on *The Meaning of Prayer,* which is filled with Bible references pertaining to prayer. She recommended several books on the life of Jesus Christ which also are filled with Bible references. She recommended life-changing books by Sam Shoemaker and others. These titles spell out appropriate Bible sources for the very spiritual ideas Rev. Shoemaker was teaching early AAs. So too with the Glenn Clark books and E. Stanley Jones books.

Begin by looking at *The Greatest Thing in the World* by Drummond, which discusses 1 Corinthians 13. Then, you'll look at several commentaries on Matthew Chapters 5-7 (containing the actual sermon on the mount delivered by Jesus). These include books by Oswald Chambers, Glenn Clark, E. Stanley Jones, Emmet Fox, Robert E. Speer, Emmet Fox, and others. Most of those authors discuss almost every single verse in the sermon. Though there is no commentary on the Book of James, *The Runner's Bible* (which Dr. Bob widely recommended) discusses many parts of James--the book Anne frequently read to Bob and Bill at the Smith home in the summer of 1935. The many books by Rev. Sam Shoemaker, Oxford Group writers, New Thought writers, and others such as Toyohiko Kagawa and Glenn Clark all became rich sources for the simple ideas AAs extracted from the Good Book and incorporated into their spiritual program of recovery. That program, of course, involved intensive work with newcomers, prayer, Bible study, and daily fellowship with like-minded believers.

Verses That Received Special Attention and Use

- **The Creator: "In the beginning, God created..." (Genesis 1:1)**

- **The Ten Commandments (Exodus 20:1-17)**

- **"Speak, LORD; for thy servant heareth" (1 Samuel 3:9)**

- **"The LORD is my shepherd..." (all of Psalm 23)**

- **".... I will say of the LORD, He is my refuge and my fortress: my God; in him will I trust..." (all of Psalm 91)**

- **"Trust in the LORD with all thine heart..." (all of Proverbs 3:5-6)**

- "Therefore if thou bring thy gift to the altar..." (all of Matthew 5:23-24)

- "Agree with thine adversary quickly..." (all of Matthew 5:25)

- "After this manner therefore pray ye: Our Father which art in heaven... (all of the Lord's prayer in Matthew 6:9-13)

- "But seek ye first the kingdom of God, and his righteousness; and all these things shall be added unto you" (Matthew 6:33)

- "And why beholdest thou the mote that is thy brother's eye, but considerest not the beam in thine own eye..." (all of Matthew 7:3-5)

- "Therefore all things whatsoever ye would that men should do to you, do even so to them: for this is the law and the prophets" (Matthew 7:12)

- "Ask and it shall be given you; seek, and ye shall find..." (Matthew 7:7-12)

- "Not every one that saith unto me, Lord, Lord, shall enter into the kingdom of heaven; but he that doeth the will of my Father which is in heaven" (Matthew 7:21)

- "Jesus said unto him, Thou shalt love the Lord thy God with all thy heart, and with all thy mind. This is the first and great commandment. And the second is like unto it, Thou shalt love thy neighbor as thyself" (Matthew 22:36-40)

- "For God so loved the world, that he gave his only begotten Son, that whosoever believeth in him should not perish, but have everlasting life" (John 3:16)

- "But ye shall receive power, after that the Holy Ghost is come upon you: and ye shall be witnesses unto me both in Jerusalem, and in Judea, and in Samaria, and unto the uttermost part of the earth" (Acts 1:8)

- "And be not conformed to this world: but be ye transformed by the renewing of your mind, that ye may prove what is that good, and acceptable, and perfect, will of God" (Romans 12:1-2)

- "That if thou shalt confess with thy mouth the Lord Jesus, and shalt believe in thine heart that God hath raised him from the dead, thou shalt be saved" (Romans 10:9)

- "Though I speak with the tongues of men and angels, and have not charity…" (all of 1 Corinthians 13:1-13)

- "Let love be without dissimulation. Abhor that which is evil; cleave to that which is good" (Romans 12:9)

- "But without faith it is impossible to please him: for he that cometh to God must believe that he is, and that he is a rewarder of them that diligently seek him" (Hebrews 11:6)

- "He that loveth not knoweth not God; for God is love" (1 John 4:8)

- "For this is the love of God, that we keep his commandments; and his commandments are not grievous" (1 John 5:3)

The Special Role of the Books of Matthew, James, and 1 Corinthians

The focus here will be on the three portions of the Bible which Dr. Bob said he and the early A.A. pioneers considered "absolutely essential." Pointing directly to the roles of the three segments are the following pioneer comments about Matthew chapters 5-7, the Book of James, and 1 Corinthians 13:

> When we started in on Bill D. [who was A.A. Number Three], we had no Twelve Steps [said Dr. Bob]. But we were convinced that the answer to our problems was in the Good Book. To some of us older ones, the parts that we found absolutely essential were the Sermon on the Mount, the thirteenth chapter of First Corinthians, and the Book of James (*The Co-founders of Alcoholics Anonymous: Biographical sketches Their last major talks*,1972, 1975, pp. 9-10).

> [Dr. Bob said, in Youngstown, Ohio:] Members of Alcoholics Anonymous begin the day with a prayer for strength and a short period of Bible reading. They find the basic messages they need in the Sermon on the Mount, in Corinthians and the Book of James (Wally P., *But for the Grace of God,* p. 45).

> [Dr. Bob's son "Smitty" recently recalled:] Before there was a Big Book—in the period of "flying blind," God's Big Book was the reference used in our home. The summer of 1935,

when Bill lived with us, Dr. Bob had read the Bible completely three times. And the references that seemed consistent with the program goals were the Sermon on the Mount, I Corinthians 13, and the Book of James (Dick B., *The Good Book and The Big Book,* p. ix).

[An early pamphlet commissioned by Dr. Bob stated:] There is the Bible that you haven't opened for years. Get acquainted with it. Read it with an open mind. You will find things that will amaze you. You will be convinced that certain passages were written with you in mind. Read the Sermon on the Mount (Matthew V, VI, and VII). Read St. Paul's inspired essay on love (I Corinthians XIII). Read the Book of James. Read the Twenty-third and Ninety-first Psalms. These readings are brief but so important (*A Manual for Alcoholics Anonymous,* rev ed., AA of Akron, 1989, p. 8).

[Bill Wilson said of his stay with Dr. Bob and Anne for three months in 1935:] Each morning there was devotion. After the long silence Anne [Dr. Bob's wife] would read out of the Good Book. James was our favorite (*RHS.* New York: The AA Grapevine, Inc., 1951, p. 5).

The definition of love in Corinthians also played a great part in our discussions (Kurtz, *Not-God.* Hazelden, 1991, p. 320, n. 11).

The Sermon on the Mount [Matthew chapters 5-7] contains the underlying spiritual philosophy of A.A. [said both Bill Wilson and Dr. Bob] (Dick B., *The Good Book and The Big Book: A.A.'s Roots in the Bible,* p. 4).

The key Bible segments, then–considered absolutely essential in putting together A.A.'s spiritual program of recovery–were the Sermon, James, and 1 Corinthians 13.

And there seems little doubt that any purportedly accurate, comprehensive, and fair study of A.A. history, A.A. principles, A.A. literature, and the A.A. fellowship requires a knowledge of what the early AAs took from the three key Bible sources. Those three segments of Biblical materials clearly influenced or found their way into the Big Book and the Twelve Steps. And those Bible segments are of such historical significance that they justify the following, separate, item-by-item review.

The Sermon on the Mount (Matthew 5-7)

This discussion will not deal with a particular book or commentary on Matthew chapters 5-7. It will focus on the Sermon on the Mount itself; for this Sermon, which Jesus delivered, was not the property of some present-day commentator or writer. The fact that Dr. Bob read the Matthew chapters *themselves,* as well as many interpretations of them, verifies the A.A. belief that the Sermon was one of the principles comprising "the common property of mankind," which Bill Wilson said the AAs had borrowed. And here are some major points that appear to have found their way from the Sermon into the basic ideas of the Big Book. The points were, of course, in the sermon itself. In addition, the pioneers read many books and articles on and about the sermon which are thoroughly documented in the author's title, *The Good Book and The Big Book: A.A.'s Roots in the Bible.* Those items further illustrate some of the points made in the sermon and that might have found their way into A.A.

The Lord's Prayer—Matthew 6:9-13

Oxford Group meetings closed with the Lord's Prayer in New York and in Akron. In early A.A., they also closed meetings with the Lord's Prayer. Moreover, the author has attended at least two thousand A.A. meetings, and almost every one has closed with the Lord's Prayer. At the 1990 International A.A. Conference in Seattle, which was a first for this author, some 50,000 members of Alcoholics Anonymous joined in closing their meetings with the Lord's Prayer. The question here concerns what parts, if any, of the Lord's Prayer found their way into the Big Book, Twelve Steps, A.A. Slogans, and the A.A. fellowship; and we hasten to remind the reader that the prayer is *part of the Sermon on the Mount.* Here are the verses of the Lord's Prayer (*King James Version*) as found in Matt. 6:9-13. Jesus instructed the Judaeans, "After this manner therefore pray ye":

> Our Father which art in heaven, Hallowed be thy name. Thy kingdom come. Thy will be done in earth, as *it is* in heaven. Give us this day our daily bread.

And forgive us our debts, as we forgive our debtors.
And lead us not into temptation, but deliver us from evil: For thine is the kingdom, and the power, and the glory, for ever. Amen.

Dr. Bob studied specific commentaries on the Sermon by Oswald Chambers, Glenn Clark, Emmet Fox, and E. Stanley Jones. And these writers extracted a good many teachings, prayer guides, and theological ideas from Lord's Prayer verses in the Sermon. But there are a few concepts and phrases in the Lord's Prayer itself which either epitomize A.A. thinking or can be found in its language—whether the A.A. traces came from the Lord's Prayer or from other portions of the Bible. For example, the Big Book uses the word "Father" when referring to the Creator Yahweh, our God; and the context shows that this usage and name came from the Bible. The Oxford Group also used the term "Father," among other names, when referring to God. The concept and expression of God as "Father" is not confined to the Sermon on the Mount. It can be found in many other parts of the New Testament. But AAs have given the "Our Father" prayer a special place in their meetings. Thus the Lord's Prayer seems the likely source of their use of the word "Father."

The phrase "Thy will be done" is directly quoted, or is the specific subject of reference, in the Big Book several times (Big Book, 4th ed., pp. 63, 67, 76, 85, 88). It underlies A.A.'s contrast between "self-will" and "God's will." The Oxford Group stressed, as do A.A.'s Third and Seventh Step prayers, that there must be a *decision to do God's will and surrender to His will*. These ideas were also symbolized in the A.A. prayer's "Thy will be done."

Finally, "Forgive us our debts" or "trespasses" certainly states that God can and will "forgive"; and these concepts can be found in the Big Book, whether they came from the Lord's Prayer or from other important Biblical sources such as the Book of James.

The Full "Sermon on the Mount": Matthew Chapters 5-7

Dr. Bob studied, and circulated among early AAs, an E. Stanley Jones book, *The Christ of the Mount* (Nashville: Abingdon, 1931; Festival ed., 1985, pp. 36-37) which outlined the Sermon's contents in this fashion:

1. The goal of life: To be perfect or complete as the Father in heaven is perfect or complete (5:48); with twenty-seven marks of this perfect life (5:1-47).

   [Jones wrote of these verses:] The perfect life consists in being poor in spirit, in mourning, in being meek, in hungering and thirsting after righteousness, in being merciful, pure in heart, in being a peacemaker, persecuted for righteousness sake and yet rejoicing and being exceeding glad, in being the salt of the earth, the light of the world, having a righteousness that exceeds, in being devoid of anger with the brother, using no contemptuous words, allowing no one to hold anything against one, having the spirit of quick agreement, no inward lustful thinking, relentless against anything that offends against the highest, right relations in the home life, truth in speech and attitude, turning the other cheek, giving the cloak also, going the second mile, giving to those who ask and from those who would borrow turning not away, loving even one's enemies, praying for those that persecute (pp. 50-51).

2. A diagnosis of the reason why men do not reach or move on to that goal: Divided personality (6:1-6; 7:1-6).

3. The Divine offer of an adequate moral and spiritual re-enforcement so that men can move on to that goal: The Holy Spirit to them that ask him (7:7-11).

4. After making the Divine offer he gathers up and emphasizes in two sentences our part in reaching that goal. Toward others we are to do unto others as we would that they should do unto us (7:12); toward ourselves—we are to lose ourselves by entering the straight gate (7:13).

5. The test of whether we are moving on to that goal, or whether this Divine Life is operative within us: By their fruits (7:15-23).

6. The survival value of this new life and the lack of survival value of life lived in any other way: The house founded on rock and the house founded on sand (7:24-27).

Our own discussion will review Jesus's Sermon, chapter by chapter. It will pinpoint some principal thoughts that Dr. Bob and Bill may have had in mind when they each said that the sermon on the mount contained the underlying philosophy of Alcoholics Anonymous. Here follows our review. And see also my new title *The James Club and The Original A.A. Program's Absolute Essentials.*

Matthew Chapter 5

1. **The Beatitudes**. The Beatitudes are found in Matt. 5:3-11. The word "beatitudes" refers to the first word "Blessed" in each of these verses. Merriam Webster's says "blessed" means "enjoying the bliss of heaven." The word in the Greek New Testament from which "blessed" was translated means, "happy," accoring Biblical scholar Ethelbert Bullinger. *Vine's Expository Dictionary of Old and New Testament Words* explains the word "Blessed" as follows: "In the beatitudes the Lord indicates not only the characters that are blessed, but the nature of that which is the highest good." Dr. Bob's wife Anne Smith described the Beatitudes in the Sermon on the Mount as "the Christ-like virtues to be cultivated" (Dick B., *Anne Smith's Journal,* p. 135).

The beatitude verses can be found at the very beginning of Jesus's sermon and read as follows:

> And seeing the multitudes, he went up into a mountain: and when he was set, his disciples came unto him:
> And he opened his mouth, and taught them, saying,
> Blessed are the poor in spirit: for theirs is the kingdom of heaven.
> Blessed are they that mourn: for they shall be comforted.
> Blessed are the meek: for they shall inherit the earth.
> Blessed are they which do hunger and thirst after righteousness: for they shall be filled.
> Blessed are the merciful: for they shall obtain mercy.
> Blessed are the pure in heart: for they shall see God.
> Blessed are the peacemakers: for they shall be called the children of God.
> Blessed are they which are persecuted for righteousness' sake: for theirs is the kingdom of heaven.
> Blessed are ye, when men shall revile you, and persecute you, and shall say all manner of evil against you falsely, for my sake.
> Rejoice, and be exceeding glad: for great is your reward in heaven: for so persecuted they the prophets which were before you (Matt. 5:1-12)

Italicized below are *Webster's* definitions for the key words in each "beatitude" verse, with quotes also from the *King James Version*, which was the version Dr. Bob and early AAs most used. As the verses appear in the King James, they state: "Blessed" are:

- the poor *(humble)* in spirit [renouncing themselves, wrote E. Stanley Jones]: for theirs is the kingdom of heaven (v. 3) ;
- they that mourn *(feel or express grief or sorrow):* for they shall be comforted (v. 4);
- the meek *(enduring injury with patience and without resentment);* for they shall inherit the earth (v. 5);
- they which do hunger and thirst after righteousness *(acting in accord with divine or moral law):* for they shall be filled (v. 6);
- the merciful *(compassionate):* for they shall obtain mercy (v. 7);

- the pure *(spotless, stainless)* in heart [has a passion for righteousness and a compassion for men–seeks law and shows love, wrote Jones]: for they shall see God (v. 8);
- the peacemakers: for they shall be called the children of God (v. 9);
- they which are persecuted for righteousness sake: for theirs is the kingdom of heaven (v. 10);
- ye when men shall revile you, and persecute you, and shall say all manner of evil against you falsely, for my sake *(end or purpose):* for great is your reward in heaven: for so persecuted they the prophets which were before you (v. 11).

Did Dr. Bob, Anne, Bill, or Henrietta Seiberling study and draw specifically on these beatitude verses as they put together A.A.'s recovery program? The author can neither provide nor document an answer. But there are some ideas common to A.A.'s spiritual principles in the beatitudes as you see them expressed above. These are: (1) Humility–overcoming self; (2) Comfort for the suffering; (3) Patience and tolerance to the end of eliminating resentment; (4) Harmonizing one's actions with God's will; (5) Compassion, which *Webster* defines as "sympathetic consciousness of others distress together with a desire to alleviate;" (6) "Cleaning house"–which means seeking obedience to God and, based on the principles of love, straightening out harms caused by disobedience; (7) Making peace; (8) Standing for and acting upon spiritual principles, whatever the cost, because they are God's principles. The foregoing are Twelve Step ideas that can be found in the Beatitudes; and A.A. founders probably saw them there as well, and they can most certainly be found in the Big Book–humility, comforting others, patience and tolerance, "Thy will be done," compassion, amends, peacemaking, acting on the "cardinal principles of Jesus Christ" as virtues to be cultivated.

2. **Letting your light shine**. Matt. 5:13-16 suggest glorifying your Heavenly Father by letting others *see* your good works. That is, "Letting your light shine" does not mean glorifying yourself, but rather glorifying God by letting others see your spiritual walk *in action*—see the immediate results of surrender to the Master. These ideas may be reflected in the Big Book's statement: "Our real purpose is to fit ourselves to be of maximum service to God. . . ." (p. 77).

3. **Obeying the Ten Commandments**. In Matt. 5:17-21, Jesus reiterates the importance of obeying the law and the prophets, specifically referring to Exod. 20:13 (Thou shalt not kill), but obviously referring to the other important commandments such as having no other god but Yahweh (Exod. 20:2-3), worshiping no other god (Exod. 20:4-5), eschewing adultery (Exod. 20:14), not stealing (Exod. 20:15), and so on. And even though some of these commandments may have fallen between the cracks in today's A.A., they very clearly governed the moral standards of early A.A. that Dr. Bob and the Akron AAs embraced. The Ten Commandments were part of early A.A. pamphlets and literature, and (for example) Dr. Bob and the Akron AAs would have nothing to do with a man who was committing adultery.

4. **The Law of Love in action**. In Matt. 5:17-47, Jesus confirms that the Law of Love fulfills the Old Testament Law. He rejects anger without cause, unresolved wrongs to a brother, quibbling with an adversary, lust and impurity, adultery, retaliation, and hatred of an enemy. The author's title *The Oxford Group & Alcoholics Anonymous* covers many of these ideas as roots of A.A. principles. And the foregoing verses in Matthew may very well have influenced A.A. language about: (1) Overcoming resentments [". . .I say unto you, That whosoever is angry with his brother without a cause shall be in danger of the judgment. . .]; (2) Making restitution ["Therefore if thou bring thy gift before the altar, and there rememberest that thy brother hath ought against thee; Leave there thy gift before the altar, and go thy way; first be reconciled to thy brother, and then come and offer thy gift"]; (3) Avoidance of retaliation for wrongdoing by others ["Ye have heard that it hath been said, An eye for an eye, and a tooth for a tooth: But I say unto you, That ye resist not evil: but whosoever shall smite thee on thy right cheek, turn to him the other also"]; and (4) Making peace with our enemies ["Ye have heard that it hath been said, Thou shalt love thy neighbor, and hate thine enemy. But I say unto you. Love your enemies, bless them that curse you, do good to them that hate you, and pray for them which despitefully use you, and persecute you"]

Matthew Chapter 6

1. **Anonymity**. Matt. 6:1-8, 16-18 (urging almsgiving "in secret," praying "in secret," fasting "in secret," and avoiding "vain repetitions," and hypocrisy) very possibly played a role in the development of A.A.'s spiritual principle of anonymity. Jesus said, "your Father knoweth what things ye have need of, before ye ask him" and "thy Father, which seeth in secret. shall reward thee openly." The vain practices which Jesus condemned were focused on one's inflating the ego and focus on self-centeredness--something A.A. disdains. Early Oxford Group and A.A. literature often spoke of "God-sufficiency" versus "self-sufficiency," and "God-centeredness" versus "self-centeredness" and "ego-centricity." We have located no direct tie between the teachings of Jesus on anonymity and A.A.'s traditions on this "spiritual" principle. But the concepts are parallel; and *The Runner's Bible* and other A.A. biblical sources that AAs studied do discuss their significance at some length.

2. **Forgiveness**. Matt. 6:14-15 refer to forgiving men their trespasses; and Emmet Fox's forceful writing about these verses may well have influenced the A.A. amends process. Fox said:

> The forgiveness of sins is the central problem of life. . . . It is, of course, rooted in selfishness. . . . We must positively and definitely extend forgiveness to everyone to whom it is possible that we can owe forgiveness, namely, to anyone who we think can have injured us in any way. . . When you hold resentment against anyone, you are bound to that person by a cosmic link, a real, tough metal chain. You are tied by a cosmic tie to the thing that you hate. The one person perhaps in the whole world whom you most dislike is the very one to whom you are attaching yourself by a hook that is stronger than steel (Fox, *The Sermon on the Mount*, pp. 183-88).

There is no assurance that Fox's writing on this sermon forgiveness point specifically influenced the Big Book's emphasis on forgiveness. To be sure, at least two A.A. history writers have claimed that Fox's writings did influence Bill Wilson. However, other books that were read by early AAs–books by such authors as Henry Drummond, Glenn Clark, E. Stanley Jones, and Harry Emerson Fosdick–used language similar to that used by Fox in his discussion of forgiveness of enemies. And Jesus' sermon on the mount is not the only place in the New Testament where forgiveness is stressed. Thus, after, and even though, Christ had accomplished remission of past sins of believers, Paul wrote:

> Forbearing one another, and forgiving one another, if any man have a quarrel against any: even as Christ forgave you, so also *do ye* (Col. 3:13)

See also the following verse, a favorite often quoted and used by Henrietta Seiberling–a well known early A.A. teacher who was often thought of as an A.A. founder:

> If a man say I love God, and hateth his brother. he is a liar: for he that loveth not his brother whom he hath seen, how can he love God whom he hath not seen? (1 John 4:20)

In any event, the Big Book, Third Edition, states at page 77:

> The question of how to approach the man we hated will arise. It may be he has done us more harm than we have done him and, though we may have acquired a better attitude toward him, we are still not too keen about admitting our faults. Nevertheless, with a person we dislike, we take the bit in our teeth. It is harder to go to an enemy than to a friend, but we find it more beneficial to us. We go to him in a helpful *and forgiving spirit,* confessing our former ill feeling and expressing our regret. Under no condition do we criticize such a person or argue. Simply we tell him that we will never get over drinking until we have done our utmost to straighten out the past (italics added).

3. **"The sunlight of the Spirit?"** Speaking of the futility and unhappiness in a life which includes deep resentment, the Big Book states: "when harboring such feelings we shut ourselves off from the sunlight of the Spirit." One often hears this "sunlight" expression quoted in A.A. meetings. Yet its origins seem unreported and undocumented. Anne Smith referred frequently in her journal to the verses in 1 John which had to do with fellowship with God and walking in the light as God is light. So did A.A.'s Oxford Group sources. And the following are the most frequently quoted verses from

1 John having to do with God as "light" and the importance of walking in the light (rather than walking in darkness) in order to have fellowship with Him:

> That which we have seen and heard declare we unto you, that ye may have fellowship with us: and truly our fellowship *is* with the Father, and with his Son, Jesus Christ. And these things write we unto you, that your joy may be full.
> This then is the message which we have heard of him, and declare unto you, that God is light, and in him is no darkness at all. If we say that we have fellowship with him, and walk in darkness, we lie, and do not the truth:
> But if we walk in the light, as he is in the light, we have fellowship one with another, and the blood of Jesus Christ his Son cleanseth us from all sin (1 John 1:3-7).

Though this particular discussion is concerned with the Sermon on the Mount, we have mentioned also the foregoing verses from 1 John 1:3-7 (having to do with walking in God's light as against opposed to walking in darkness). For very possibly those ideas in 1 John, together with the following verses in the Sermon, may have given rise to Bill's references to the alcoholic's being blocked from the "sunlight of the Spirit" when he or she dwells in such dark realms as excessive anger. Matt. 6:22-24 (in the Sermon) state:

> The light of the body is the eye: if therefore thine eye be single, thy whole body shall be full of light. But if thine eye be evil, thy whole body shall be full of darkness. If therefore the light that is in thee be darkness, how great *is* that darkness! No man can serve two masters: for either he will hate the one, and love the other: or else he will hold to the one, and despise the other. Ye cannot serve God and mammon.

4. Seek ye first the kingdom of God. Matt. 6:24-34 seem to have had tremendous influence on A.A. They begin with the statements:

> No man can serve two masters: for either he will hath the one, and love the other; or else he will hold to the one, and despise the other. Ye cannot serve God and mammon.

The substance of the next verses is that man need not be anxious about his life, his food, his drink, his body, or his clothing because all these needs will be taken care of when he gets his priorities straight and seeks *first* the kingdom of God and His righteousness. Verse 33 then says:

> But seek ye first the kingdom of God, and his righteousness; and all these things [food. clothing, and shelter] shall be added unto you.

Dr. Bob specifically explained the origin of our A.A. slogans "Easy Does It" and "First Things First." *(DR. BOB and the Good Oldtimers,* pp 135, 144). When he was asked the meaning of "First Things First," Dr. Bob replied. "Seek ye first the kingdom of God and His righteousness, and all these things shall be added unto you." He told his sponsee Clarence S. that "First Things First" came from Matt. 6:33 in the sermon on the mount. And this verse was widely quoted in the books that Dr. Bob and the Akron AAs read and recommended (Dick B., *The Good Book and The Big Book,* p. 125, n.119; *That Amazing Grace,* pp. 30, 38).

On page 60, the Big Book states the A.A. solution for relief from alcoholism: "God could and would if He were sought." This concept of "seeking" results by reliance on God instead of reliance on self is a bedrock idea in the Big Book (see Third Edition, pp. 11, 14, 25, 28, 43, 52-53, 57, 62). In view of Dr. Bob's explanations as to the origin of "First Things First," the Big Book's emphasis on "seeking" very likely came from the "seeking the kingdom of God first" idea in Matt. 6:33.

According to Dr. Bob, the slogans "Easy Does It" and "One day at a time" came from the next verse–Matthew 6:34. See Dick B., *The Good Book and The Big Book,* pp. 87-88, and other citations therein.

Matthew Chapter 7

1. **Taking your own inventory**. Much of A.A.'s Fourth, Ninth, Tenth, and Eleventh Step actions involve looking for your own part, for your own fault in troublesome matters. This self-examination process (as part of the house-cleaning and life-changing process in the Steps) was expected to result in that which, in Appendix II of the Third Edition of the Big Book, became described as "the personality change sufficient to bring about recovery from alcoholism" (Big Book, p. 569). Matt. 7:3-5 states:

> And why beholdest thou the mote [speck] that is in thy brother's eye, but considerest not the beam [log] that is in thine own eye?
> Or how wilt thou say to thy brother, Let me pull the mote [speck] out of thine eye; and, behold, a beam [log] *is* in thine own eye.
> Thou hypocrite, first cast out the beam [log] out of thine own eye; and then shalt thou see clearly to cast out the mote [speck] out of thy brother's eye.

These verses from Matthew were frequently cited by A.A.'s spiritual sources as the Biblical foundation for self-examination and thus finding one's own part, one's own erroneous conduct, in a relationship problem.

2. **Ask, seek, knock**. Matt. 7:7-11 states:

> Ask, and it shall be given you; seek, and ye shall find; knock, and it shall be opened unto you;
> For every one that asketh receiveth; and he that seeketh findeth; and to him that knocketh it shall be opened. Or what man is there of you, whom if his son ask bread, will he give him a stone? Or if he ask a fish, will he give him a serpent?
> If ye then, being evil, know how to give good gifts unto your children, how much more shall your Father which is in heaven give good things to them that ask him?

Bill Wilson's spiritual teacher, Rev. Sam Shoemaker, wrote:

> Our part [in the crisis of self-surrender] is to ask, to seek, to knock. His [God's] part is to answer, to come, to open (Shoemaker, *Realizing Religion,* p. 32).

The Runner's Bible (one of the most important of the early A.A. Bible devotionals) has an entire chapter titled, "Ask and Ye shall receive." Another favored devotional among the A.A. pioneers was *My Utmost for His Highest,* by Oswald Chambers. Chambers says, about the foregoing verses beginning with Matt. 7:7:

> The illustration of prayer that Our Lord uses here is that of a good child asking for a good thing. . . . It is no use praying unless we are living as children of God. Then, Jesus says: "Everyone that asketh receiveth."

The foregoing verses, and relevant comments by A.A. sources, underline the importance of becoming a child of God, establishing a harmonious relationship with Him, and *then* expecting good results from the Creator, Yahweh, our God–"Providence" from Him as our Heavenly Father. Given the emphasis in early A.A. on the Sermon, those verses from Matt. 7 very probably influenced the following similar ideas expressed as follows in the Big Book's Third Edition and Fourth Edition:

> If what we have learned and felt and seen means anything at all, it means that all of us, whatever our race, creed, or color are the children of a living Creator with whom we may form a relationship upon simple and understandable terms as soon as we are willing and honest enough to try (p. 28).

> God will constantly disclose more to you and to us. Ask Him in your morning meditation what you can do each day for the man who is still sick. The answers will come, *if your own house is in order.* But obviously you cannot transmit something you haven't got. See *to it that your relationship with Him is right,* and great events will come to pass for you and countless others. This is the Great Fact for us (p. 164, italics added).

In this same vein. Dr. Bob's wife, Anne, wrote, in the spiritual journal she shared with early AAs and their families:

> We can't give away what we haven't got. We must have a genuine contact with God in our present experience. Not an experience of the past, but an experience in the present—actual, genuine (Dick B., *Anne Smith's Journal*, p. 121).

3. **Do unto others**. The so-called "Golden Rule" cannot, as such, be readily identified in A.A.'s Big Book though it certainly is a much-quoted portion of the sermon on the mount which Bill and Dr. Bob said underlies A.A.'s philosophy. The relevant verse is Matt. 7:12:

> Therefore all things whatsoever ye would that men should do to you, do ye even so to them: for this is the law and the prophets.

Perhaps the following two Big Book segments bespeak that philosophy as Bill may have seen it:

> We have begun to learn tolerance, patience and good will toward all men, even our enemies, for we look on them as sick people. We have listed the people we have hurt by our conduct, and are willing to straighten out the past if we can (p. 70).

> Then you will know what it means to give of yourself that others may survive and rediscover life. You will learn the full meaning of "Love thy neighbor as thyself" (p. 153).

4. **He that doeth the will of my Father**. There are *several* key verses in the sermon on the mount which could have caused Bob and Bill to say that Matthew Chapters Five to Seven contained A.A.'s underlying philosophy. The verses are in the Lords Prayer itself (Matt. 6:9-13), the so-called Golden Rule quoted above (Matt. 7:12), and the phrase "Thy will be done" (Matt. 6:10). In addition to these three roots, however, I believe that the major spiritual principle borrowed by the founders from the sermon on the mount—can be found in Matt. 7:21:

> Not every one that saith unto me. Lord, Lord, shall enter into the kingdom of heaven; but he that doeth the will of my Father which is in heaven.

Bill Wilson said clearly in the Big Book and in his other writings that the key to success in A.A. is doing the will of the Father–the Father Who is the *subject* of the Lord's Prayer, Almighty God Whose will was to be done, and the Creator upon whom early AAs relied. Note that Wilson wrote:

> I was to sit quietly when in doubt, asking only for direction and strength to meet my problems as He would have me (Bill's Story, Big Book, 4th ed., p. 13).

> He humbly offered himself to his Maker—then he knew (Big Book, 4th ed., p. 57).

> . . . praying only for knowledge of His will for us and the power to carry that out (Step Eleven, Big Book, 4th ed., p. 59).

> May I do Thy will always (portion of "Third Step Prayer," Big Book, 4th ed., p. 63)!

> Thy will be done (Big Book, 4th ed, pp. 67, 88).

> Grant me strength, as I go out from here, to do your bidding. Amen (portion of "Seventh Step Prayer," Big Book, 4th ed., p. 76).

> There is God, our Father, who very simply says, 'I am waiting for you to do my will' *(Alcoholics Anonymous Comes of Age,* p. 105).

The Book of James

Of probably even greater importance (than the Sermon) in the day-by-day thinking of early A.A. was the Book of James. It was much studied by A.A.'s co-founders. Quotes and ideas from the Apostle

James can be found throughout the Big Book and in A.A. literature. The Book of James was considered so important that many favored calling the A.A. fellowship the "James Club" *(DR. BOB and the Good Oldtimers,* p. 71; *Pass It On,* p. 147). And even the most fundamental phrases in A.A., such as "It Works" and Bill Wilson's own "Works Publishing Company" (which published the First Edition of the Big Book), probably have their origin in the "Faith without works is dead" phrases in the Book of James (See: Nell Wing, *Grateful to Have Been There,* pp. 70-71).

Let's therefore review the Book of James, chapter by chapter. As we do so, we will point to traces of that book which we believe can be found in, or probably influenced the text of, the Big Book. At the outset, we would report that as our research into the Biblical roots of A.A. has progressed, so has our understanding of some root sources that previously went unnoticed.

For example, some time back, Dr. Bob's son, Robert R. Smith, told the author by phone that his father had placed great stake in *The Runner's Bible.* We had encountered difficulty locating a copy. And we were still looking for some commentary on the Book of James similar to the many on the sermon on the mount (by Oswald Chambers, Glenn Clark, Emmet Fox, and E. Stanley Jones) and on 1 Corinthians 13 (by Henry Drummond, for example). And Dr. Bob extensively studied and circulated most of these among the Pioneers. We believed such above-mentioned commentaries probably impacted upon the thinking of Dr. Bob, Anne, Henrietta, and the early AAs just as the actual Bible verses in Matthew chapters 5-7 and 1 Corinthians 13 have.

But we could find no similar commentary that the pioneers used with the Book of James, despite A.A.'s specific emphasis on James. Finally, as we studied the spiritual literature early AAs read, we noticed in *The Runner's Bible* the frequency with which all the books and chapters that Dr. Bob called "absolutely essential" (Matthew chapters 5-7, 1 Corinthians 13, and James) were there mentioned. We particularly noticed the frequency with which *The Runner's Bible* mentioned and discussed verses from the Book of James. Hence our reader will find many references to *The Runner's Bible* in the footnotes of our title *The Good Book and The Big Book;* for we believe that the little "Runner's" devotional book may have provided Dr. Bob, Anne Smith, and perhaps even Bill Wilson, with much of the fodder that caused them to focus on James and conclude that James was their "favorite" book of the Bible.

In a phone conversation with the author in 1995, from his home in Texas, Dr. Bob's son stated he felt it would be almost impossible for him, at this late date, to confirm that *The Runner's Bible* was the source of either A.A.'s or its founders' emphasis on James or other parts of the Bible. But he pointed out that the little Biblical devotional book was used by those who wanted a quick and easy source for Biblical ideas in which they were interested. This leads me to believe that the Runner's book became a reference source for Dr. Bob, Anne, and even Bill Wilson when they were studying the pertinent Biblical ideas they extracted from 1 Corinthians 13, the Sermon on the Mount, and particularly James. Now let's look at the chapters in James–one by one.

James Chapter 1

1. **Patience**. Chapter One is not the only chapter in the Book of James which mentions patience. Nor is it the only portion of the Bible that stresses patience. But we've noted that James was a favored Biblical source in early A.A., and James 1:3-4 do state:

> Knowing *this,* that the trying of your faith worketh patience. But let patience have *her* perfect work, that ye may be perfect and entire, wanting nothing.

Patience certainly wound up as one of the most frequently mentioned spiritual principles in the Big Book (pp. 67, 70, 83, 111, 118, 163).

2. **Asking wisdom of God with unwavering believing**. James 1:5-8 state:

> If any of you lack wisdom, let him ask of God, that giveth to all *men* liberally, and upbraideth not; and it shall be given him.But let him ask in faith, nothing wavering. For he that wavereth is like a wave of the sea driven with the wind and tossed. For let not that man think that he shall receive anything of the Lord. A double minded man *is* unstable in all his ways.

Asking for God's direction and strength and receiving "Guidance" from Him, are major themes in both the Old and New Testaments. They were important Oxford Group ideas as well. We therefore discussed them at length in our titles on the Oxford Group and on Anne Smith's spiritual journal. Certainly the Big Book, including the Eleventh Step itself, is filled with such Guidance concepts (3rd ed., pp.13, 46, 49, 62-63, 69-70, 76, 79-80, 83, 84-88, 100, 117, 120, 124, 158, 164).

3. **Resisting temptation**. It should surprise no one that AAs of yesteryear and of today are interested in resisting temptation, and having the power to do that—the power of God. James 1:12-16 state:

> Blessed *is* the man that endureth temptation: for when he is tried, he shall receive the crown of life, which the Lord hath promised to those that love him.
> Let no man say when he is tempted, I am tempted of God: for God cannot be tempted with evil, neither tempteth he any man:
> But every man is tempted when he is drawn away of his own lust and enticed.
> Then when lust bath conceived, it bringeth forth sin: and sin, when it is finished, bringeth forth death.
> Do not err, my beloved brethren.

[My personal view is that the foregoing verses offer much insight for the cure of alcoholism and other life-controlling afflictions.

Man is to resist the devil–says James in a later verse. Man is to endure temptation when he is tried. When he is tempted, he cannot blame the temptation on God–who cannot be tempted and does not tempt. He can be tempted by being drawn away of his own lust and enticed. James 3:15-16 speaks of a "wisdom [that] descendeth not from above, but is earthly, sensual, and devilish." And, says James, when the enticement results in lustful [and excessive] thoughts and behavior [such as getting drunk and drunkenness], it can and should be recognized as sin, and sin as the producer of death. For the real alcoholic, the devilish thoughts must be expelled.

The prescription is not merely to abstain from drinking and go to 12 Step meetings. The enjoined error occurs when the man fails to submit to God, resist the devil, humble himself in the sight of God, and appropriately believe to be lifted up and out by his Creator. 2 Corinthians 10:5 calls for casting down human reasoning and "every high thing that exalteth itself against the knowledge of God, and bringing into captivity every thought to the obedience of Christ." We are the ones to control the thoughts. 1 Corinthians 10:13 points out: "There hath no temptation taken you but such as is common to man; but God is faithful, who will not suffer you to be tempted above that ye are able; but will with the temptation also make a way to escape, that ye may be able to bear it."

To be "cured," I believe, we need to recognize that temptation to disobey God is common and that letting the temptation thoughts make a nest in our mind and motivate our actions must be cast out. They need to be resisted. Man needs to stand against the devil. His thoughts need to be expelled. And we need to believe what God says–we are submit ourselves to God; resist the devil; and be assured that the devil will flee. We also need to believe that when we humble ourselves and turn to Him, God will lift us up. And we need to believe, without doubting, and that we can bear and escape the temptation with the help of our faithful Creator.]

4. Every good and perfect gift comes from God, the Father of lights. James 1:17 states:

> Every good gift and every perfect gift is from above, and cometh down from the Father of lights, with whom is no variableness, neither shadow of turning.

Bill seemed to be referring to this verse when he wrote on page 14 of *Alcoholics Anonymous*, 4th ed.:

> I must turn in all things to the Father of Light [sic] who presides over us all. [Alcoholics Anonymous, 1st ed., has "the Father of Lights," p. 23.]

Bill made the same reference to God, the Father of lights, who presides over us all, in Appendix I of *Alcoholics Anonymous*, 4th ed.:

> This to the end that our great blessings may never spoil us; that we shall forever live in thankful contemplation of Him who presides over us all (p. 566).

The "Him" who presides over us all was, of course, James 1:17's "Father of lights"— the Creator Yahweh, our Almighty God.

5. Let every man be slow to speak, slow to wrath. James 1:19-20 state:

> Wherefore, my beloved brethren, let every man be swift to hear, slow to speak, slow to wrath: For the wrath of man worketh not the righteousness of God.

The same verse is quoted in *The Runner's Bible* and seems quite relevant to the Big Book's injunction, "If we were to live, we had to be free of anger. . . . God save me from being angry" (Fourth Edition, pp. 66-67).

6. Be ye doers of the word, and not hearers only. James 1:21-22 state:

> Wherefore lay apart all filthiness and superfluity of naughtiness, and receive with meekness the engrafted word, which is able to save your souls.
> But be ye doers of the word, and not hearers only, deceiving your own selves.

Reverend Sam Shoemaker made this comment on the foregoing:

> I think St. James' meaning is made much clearer in Dr. Moffatt's translation, "Act on the Word, instead of merely listening to it." Try it out in experiment, and prove it by its results—otherwise you only fool yourself into believing that you have the heart of religion when you haven't (Shoemaker, *The Gospel According to You,* pp. 44-55).

In the same chapter, Shoemaker also pointed out that prayer is often more a struggle to find God than the enjoyment of Him and cooperation with His will. He added that "God is and is a Rewarder of them that seek Him." (See *The Gospel According to You,* p. 47; and Heb. 11:6).

We cannot find specific or similar language to that of James 1:21-22 in the Big Book; but A.A. declares over and over that A.A. is a program of *action,* that probably no human power can relieve a person of his alcoholism, and "That God could and would if He were *sought"* (p. 60). A.A.'s program emphasizes action in the experiment of faith it adopted from John 7:17—*seeking* God by *following* the path that leads to a relationship with God. James 1:22 enjoins *doing* God's will as expressed in His Word—not merely listening to it. James was an Akron favorite. Shoemaker was a Wilson favorite. "Faith without works" was a Big Book favorite; and it therefore seems quite reasonable to believe and possible that A.A.'s emphasis on *action* might well have derived in part from James 1:21-22.

7. **Pure religion and undefiled before God . . . to visit the fatherless and widows in their affliction.** James 1:27 states:

> Pure religion and undefiled before God and the Father is this,
> To visit the fatherless and widows in their affliction, *and* to keep oneself unspotted from the world.

At the very least, this verse bespeaks unselfishness and helpfulness to others which were cardinal A.A. principles–particularly the principles embodied in Step Twelve. In fact, that's the point made in one of early A.A.'s pamphlets:

> And all we need to do in the St. James passage is to substitute the word "Alcoholic" for "Fatherless and Widows" and we have Step Twelve (*Spiritual Milestones*, AA of Akron, pp. 12-13).

James Chapter 2

Chapter Two of the Book of James may have made two direct and major contributions to the language of the Big Book and also to A.A.'s philosophy. Those two contributions were "Love thy neighbor as thyself" and "Faith without works is dead."

1. **Love thy neighbor as thyself.** James 2:8 states:

> If ye fulfill the royal law according to the scripture, Thou shalt love thy neighbor as thyself, ye do well.

This commandment to "Love thy neighbor" exists in other parts of both the Old and New Testaments. Thus, when the Big Book incorporated this phrase, there is no assurance that the quote is from James rather than from another Bible verse to the same effect (*e.g.*, Rom. 13:9; Gal. 5:14). But the Big Book certainly does state:

> Then you will know what it means to give of yourself that others may survive and rediscover life. You will learn the full meaning of "Love thy neighbor as thyself" (p. 153).

The Book of James is very probably the specific source of this Biblical quote since Dr. Bob, early AAs, and Bill Wilson himself spoke with such frequency about "love" and tolerance as the code of A.A. *and* the Book of James as their favorite book.

2. **Faith without works is dead.** Said to be the favorite verse of Anne Smith and perhaps the origin of many expressions in A.A. concerning "works," this sentence, or variations of it, appears several times in Chapter Two of the Book of James. For example, James 2:20 states:

> But wilt thou know, 0 vain man, that faith without works is dead?

"Faith without works" as a phrase, and as an A.A. "action" concept, is quoted or referred to many times in the Big Book (4th ed., pp. 14-15, 76, 88, 93, 97). A.A.'s original Oxford Group connection also put emphasis on these James verses, using them in connection with the importance of witnessing.

3. **Helping Others.** It hardly requires citation or documentation to state that A.A.'s cardinal objective is to help others. And this service concept is underlined in Chapter 2 of James, beginning with verses 1 to 7. James 2:15-16 state this principle very well:

> If a brother or sister be naked, and destitute of daily food, And one of you say unto them, Depart in peace, be ye warmed and filled; notwithstanding ye give them not those things which are needful to the body; what doth it profit? Even so, faith, if it hath not works, is dead, being alone.

And every alcoholic who has helped one of his miserable, suffering, destitute brothers in need will instantly relate to those verses and hence to the importance of James to the early AAs.

4. The Ten Commandments. Again! James 2:10-11 state:

> For whosoever shall keep the whole law, and yet offend in one *point,* he is guilty of all. For he that said, Do not commit adultery, said also, Do not kill. Now if thou commit no adultery, yet if thou kill, thou art become a transgressor of the law.

[Whatever one may find in today's A.A., he will find language about and references to the Ten Commandments with great frequency in *early* A.A. The Frank Amos report of 1938, quoted in this talk, is a good example.]

James Chapter 3

1. **Taming the tongue.** In his Farewell Address to A.A., Dr. Bob said:

> Let us also remember to guard that erring member the tongue, and if we must use it, let's use it with kindness and consideration and tolerance *(DR. BOB and the Good Oldtimers,* p. 338).

A major portion of James chapter 3 is devoted to the trouble that can be caused by an untamed tongue. Following are a few verses emphasizing the point:

> Even so the tongue is a little member and boasteth great things.
> Behold, how great a matter a little fire kindleth! And the tongue *is* a fire, a world of iniquity; so is the tongue among our members that it defileth the whole body, and setteth on fire the course of nature; and *it is* set on fire of hell.

> But the tongue can no man tame; it is an unruly evil, full of deadly poison.
> Out of the same mouth proceedeth blessing and cursing. My brethren, these things ought not to be (James 3:5, 6, 8, 10)

These verses are not quoted in the Big Book. But Anne Smith referred to them frequently in her journal, as did other A.A. roots sources (Dick B., *Anne Smith's Journal,* pp. 28, 44, 76, 77; Holm, *The Runner's Bible,* p. 68). But, in paraphrasing those verses, Dr. Bob seemed to be speaking of the necessity for tolerance, courtesy, consideration, and kindness in our speech and actions. James makes clear that good *conversation* should be a focus—conversation, we believe, that is laced with consideration, kindness, and tolerance (See James 3:13). And these latter principles *are* very much in evidence in the Big Book (4th ed., pp. 67, 69-70, 83-84, 97, 118, 125, 135).

2. **Avoidance of envy, strife, and lying.** James 3:14-16 proclaim that a heart filled with envy, strife, and lies has not received that kind of "wisdom" from God, but rather from devilish sources. The verses state:

> But if ye have bitter envying and strife in your hearts; glory not, and lie not against the truth.
> This wisdom descendeth not from above, but is earthly, sensual, devilish.
> For where envying and strife is, there is confusion and every evil work.

"Envy" is not as much decried in the Big Book as jealousy; but a more modern translation of these King James verses equates "envy" *with* "jealousy" (*The Revised English Bible, New Testament,* p, 208). And the Big Book most assuredly condemns jealously (4th ed., pp. 37, 69, 82, 100, 119, 145, 161). In fact, the Big Book states as to jealousy *and* envy:

> Keep it always in sight that we are dealing with that most terrible human emotion—jealousy (p. 82).

> The greatest enemies of us alcoholics are resentment, jealousy, envy, frustration, and fear (p. 145).

And as to strife, the Big Book states:

> After all, our problems were of our own making. Bottles were only a symbol. Besides, we have stopped fighting anybody or anything. We have to (p. 103)!

James 3:17-18 talk much about making peace and the fruit of righteousness being sown in peace of them that make peace.

As seen in the quote from James 3:14, lying and dishonesty are also declared to be devilish; and one should note and compare the Big Book's frequent emphasis on grasping and developing a manner of living which "demands rigorous honesty" (p. 58). As to all the verses in James 3:14-16, however, there is little certainty that these particular verses were an exclusive or even major source for the Big Books condemnation of envy, jealousy, strife, and dishonesty because all these traits are stated to be objectionable by many other parts of the Bible.

James Chapter 4:

1. **Asking amiss for selfish ends**. A.A.'s writings have much to say about overcoming selfishness and self-centeredness. But the following in James 4:3 particularly eschews selfishness in prayer:

> Ye ask, and receive not, because ye ask amiss, that ye may consume it upon your lusts.

Several Christian A.A. sources that were favorites of Dr. Bob's discuss this verse at length. And the Big Book authors may therefore have borrowed from James 4:3, in this statement:

> We ask especially for freedom from self-will, and are careful to make no request for ourselves only. We may ask for ourselves, however, if others will be helped. We are careful never to pray for our own selfish ends. Many of us have wasted a lot of time doing that and it doesn't work (Big Book, 4th ed., p. 87).

2. **Humility**. The Book of James has no corner on the Biblical injunction to be humble. But the importance of James, and the remarks

of Reverend Sam Shoemaker (quoted under Item 3 immediately below) suggest that the following verses from James may have been a source of the Big Book's frequent mention of humility. James 4:7, 10 state:

> Submit yourselves therefore to God. Resist the devil, and he will flee from you.
> Humble yourselves in the sight of the Lord, and he shall lift you up.

The Big Book's Fourth Edition is filled with exhortations to be humble, with stress on humbling one's self before God, and with suggestions for humbly asking His help. Examples include:

> There I humbly offered myself to God, as I understood Him, to do with me as He would (p. 13).

> He humbly offered himself to his Maker—then he knew (p. 57).

> Just to the extent that we do as we think He would have us, and humbly rely on Him, does He enable us to match calamity with serenity (p. 68).

> We constantly remind ourselves we are no longer running the show, humbly saying to ourselves many times each day "Thy will be done" (pp. 87-88).

3. **Trusting God and cleaning house**. James 4:8 states:

> Draw nigh to God, and he will draw nigh to you. Cleanse your hands, ye sinners; and purify your hearts, ye double minded.

The Big Book says on page 98 of the Fourth Edition:

> Burn the idea into the consciousness of every man that he can get well regardless of anyone. The only condition is that he trust in God and clean house.

And, in language closely paralleling that in James 4:8, the Big Book says further that one can establish conscious companionship with God by simply, honestly, and humbly seeking and drawing near to Him:

> He has come to all who have honestly sought Him. When we drew near to Him He disclosed Himself to us (page 57)!

In Step Seven, the Big Book relates "cleaning house" of one's character defects to "humbly asking" God to remove them. The foregoing verses in James, which speak of drawing near to God, cleansing our hearts, humbling ourselves in His sight, and then being "lifted" up by God, appear to have been directly involved in framing the Big Book's Seventh Step language. In fact, many years after the Big Book was written, Sam Shoemaker thus clarified his understanding of the Seventh Step, in a 1964 issue of the *AA Grapevine*:

> Sins get entangled deep within us, as some roots of a tree, and do not easily come loose. We need help, grace, the lift of a kind of divine derrick (Shoemaker, "Those Twelve Steps as I Understand Them"; *Volume II, Best of the Grapevine*, p. 130).

4. **Taking your own inventory**. James 4:11-12 state:

> Speak not evil one of another, brethren. He that speaketh evil of *his* brother, and judgeth his brother, speaketh evil of the law, and judgeth the law: but if thou judge the law, thou art not a doer of the law, but a judge.
> There is one lawgiver, who is able to save and to destroy: who art thou that judgest another?

We discussed the Fourth Step idea of taking your own inventory in connection with the relevant verses in the Sermon on the Mount–which were often quoted by Oxford Group people and by Anne Smith (See Matt. 7:1-5). But the Big Book also speaks of: (1) looking "for our own mistakes," (2) asking "Where were we to blame," and (3) realizing, "The inventory was ours, not the other man's." Considering the importance to AAs of the Book of James and its insights, the foregoing James verses probably also had an impact on the A.A. idea of avoiding judgment of another and focusing on an examination of one's *own* conduct when it comes to wrongdoing.

James Chapter 5

1. **Patience**. We discussed A.A.'s "patience principle" as having probably derived from James, Chapter One. As we said, however, important stress on patience can be found in James 5:7, 8, 10, 11.

2. **Grudges** (covered in A.A.'s 4th Step resentment inventory process). James 5:9 reads:

> Grudge not one against another, brethren, lest ye be condemned; behold, the judge standeth before the door.

A major portion of the Big Book's Fourth Step discussion is devoted to resentment, about which page 64 says:

> Resentment is the "number one" offender. It destroys more alcoholics than anything else. From it stem all forms of spiritual disease.

The Big Book then suggests putting resentments *on paper*—making a *"grudge list"* (pp. 64-65). Oxford Group spokesman Ebenezer Macmillan wrote at length in his title *Seeking and Finding* about eliminating resentments, hatred, or the *"grudge"* that "blocks God out effectively." Rev. Sam Shoemaker also specified "grudges" as one of the "sins" to be examined in an inventory of self (Shoemaker, *Twice-Born Ministers*, p. 182). Since the Big Book lists resentments or "grudges" as one of the four major "character defects" which block us from God, it quite possible that the "grudge" language in the Big Book was influenced by James, and perhaps specifically by James 5:9.

3. **Asking God's forgiveness for sins**. We repeat James 5:15, which was partially quoted above. The entire verse says:

> And the prayer of faith shall save the sick, and the Lord shall raise him up; and if he have committed sins, they shall be forgiven him.

The Big Book says this about asking God's forgiveness when we fall short:

> If we are sorry for what we have done, and have the honest desire to let God take us to better things, we believe we will be forgiven and will have learned our lesson (4th ed, p. 70).

> When we retire at night, we constructively review our day. . . . After making our review, we ask God's forgiveness and inquire what corrective measures should be taken (4th ed., p. 86).

The foregoing Big Book quotes show that, even after their initial surrender, wrongdoers may still, in A.A.'s view, seek and receive God's forgiveness for shortcomings indulged after the initial surrender. Here again, James has no corner on the statement that God makes it possible, through forgiveness, for a believer to regain fellowship with Him. The following in 1 John 1:9 may also have been a source of such Big Book ideas:

> If we confess our sins, he is faithful and just to forgive us *our* sins, and to cleanse us from all unrighteousness.

See also our discussion of forgiveness in connection with the Sermon on the Mount. It is fair to say, however, that the Book of James, 1 John, or Matthew could each, or all, have been the basis for the Big Book forgiveness concept.

    4. **Confess your sins one to another**. It has often been noted that *both* the Oxford Group concept of sharing by confession *and* Step Five in the Big Book were derived from James 5:16:

> Confess your faults one to another, and pray for one another, that ye may be healed.

    5. **Effectual, fervent prayer works**. James 5:16 states:

> The effectual fervent prayer of a righteous man availeth much.

A.A.'s Big Book Fourth Edition says:

> Step Eleven suggests prayer and meditation. We shouldn't be shy on this matter of prayer. Better men than we are using it constantly. It works, if we have the proper attitude and work at it.

James 5:16 could well have been a major basis for the Big Book comments on the effectiveness of prayer.

6. Anointing with oil and effecting healing through prayer by elders. See James 5:13-16.

One A.A. writer, who was sponsored by Clarence Snyder, has repeatedly suggested that in their "surrenders," early AAs almost literally followed the foregoing verses from James. Others, who also were sponsored by Clarence Snyder, have said this contention is in error. But several comments should be made about this procedure. First, there seems little confirmation that Dr. Bob, T. Henry Williams, and the Akron pioneers took the newcomer "upstairs," had him "surrender" to Christ, anointed him with oil, and prayed for him. Second, many of the elements of the James verses were followed. Third, in his later years, Clarence Snyder founded and conducted retreats for AAs and their families which are still being held. At these retreats, there is a "prayer and praise" session where there is anointing with oil and prayer for those in need. The sessions follow the close of the retreat itself. Finally, we make particular mention of these points because so many of the healing practices of the Christian church throughout later centuries did rely on the words of St. James and did heal with the laying on of hands and anointing with oil. These points are amply covered by the citation in our healing section. They are important because the convictions about "healing" and "cure" were so evident and strong in early A.A.; and the return of healing emphasis–whatever the technique or Biblical authority–is urgently needed in today's Twelve Step programs.

1 Corinthians 13

1 Corinthians 13 is often called the Bible's "love" chapter because it focuses on the importance of love in the Christian's life. In the King James Version, the word "charity" is used in the verses which are speaking of "love;" but the underlying Greek word is *agapē* which is more properly translated "love."

And the most frequently quoted characteristics of love are contained in the following verses from the King James Version of the Bible (which is the version the A.A. pioneers used):

> Charity [love] suffereth long, *and* is kind; charity envieth not; charity vaunteth not itself, is not puffed up,
> Doth not behave itself unseemly, seeketh not her own, is not easily provoked, thinketh no evil;
> Rejoiceth not in iniquity, but rejoiceth in the truth (1 Cor. 13:4-6).

The *New International Version*, which is much in use today, renders 1 Cor. 13:4-6:

> Love is patient, love is kind. It does not envy, it does not boast, it is not proud.
> It is not rude, it is not self-seeking, it is not easily angered, it keeps no record of wrongs.
> Love does not delight in evil but rejoices with the truth.

One of the most popular books in early A.A. was Professor Henry Drummond's study of 1 Corinthians 13. The title of his book, *The Greatest Thing in the World,* was taken from the last verse of 1 Corinthians chapter 13, which reads:

> And now abideth faith, hope, charity, these three; but the greatest of these is charity (1 Cor. 13:13).

Drummond's book was part of Dr. Bob's library, and a copy was still found in, and owned by, Dr. Bob's family when the author interviewed Dr. Bob's son and daughter several years ago. In much earlier years,

A.A. Old-timer Bob E. had sent a memo to Bill Wilson's wife, Lois, in which Bob E. listed *The Greatest Thing in the World* as one of three books Dr. Bob regularly provided to alcoholics with whom he worked. In fact, Dr. Bob's enthusiasm for Drummond's book is dramatized by the following remarks by a former wife of A.A. old-timer Clarence S. Clarence's former wife, Dorothy S. M., said:

> Once, when I was working on a woman in Cleveland, I called and asked him [Dr. Bob], "What do I do for somebody who is going into D.T.'s?" He told me to give her the medication, and he said, "When she comes out of it and she decides she wants to be a different woman, get her Drummond's 'The Greatest Thing in the World.' Tell her to read it through every day for 30 days, and she'll be a different woman"(See *DR. BOB and the Good Oldtimers,* p. 310).

Henry Drummond himself had made a similar suggestion half a century earlier, at the close of the lecture in which he delivered his 'greatest thing in the world' address–the address which was later published in Drummond's best-seller. Drummond said:

> Now I have all but finished. How many of you will join me in reading this chapter [1 Corinthians 13] once a week for the next three months? A man did that once and it changed his whole life. Will you do it? It is for the greatest thing in the world. You might begin by reading it every day, especially the verses which describe the perfect character. "Love suffereth long, and is kind; loveth envieth not; love vaunteth not itself." Get these ingredients into your life (See Drummond, *The Greatest Thing in the World.* p. 53).

The important influence on A.A. that came from 1 Corinthians 13 can be seen in Drummond's own simplified description of love's *ingredients*. Drummond listed nine ingredients of "love" as he saw love specifically defined in that portion of that chapter of the Bible (See Drummond, *The Greatest Thing in the World*, pp. 26-27). And we here set out those nine love ingredients with references to correlative Bible verses and correlative A.A. language:

Drummond's A.A. Big Book

Explanation Examples	Authorized KJV	NIV Version	4th ed.
1. Patience	"Charity suffereth long."	"Love is patient"	pp. 67, 70, 83, 111, 163
2. Kindness	"*and* is kind."	"love is kind"	pp. 67, 82, 83, 86
3. Generosity	"charity envieth not."	"It does not envy"	pp. 145, *cf.* 82
4. Humility	"charity vaunteth not itself" "is not puffed up.	"it does not boast, "it is not proud"	pp. 13, 57, 68, 87-88
5. Courtesy	"Doth not behave itself unseemly"	"It is not rude"	p. 69
6. Unselfishness	"seeketh not her own."	"It is not self-seeking"	pp. xxv, 93, 127
7. Good Temper	"is not easily provoked"	"it is not easily angered"	pp. 19, 67, 70, 83-
8. Guilelessness	"thinketh no evil"	"it keeps no record of wrong	84, 118, 125
9. Sincerity	"Rejoiceth not in iniquity" "but rejoiceth in the truth"	"does not delight in evil "but rejoices with the truth"	pp. xiv, xxvii, 13, 26, 28, 32, pp. 47, 55, 57-58, 63-65, 67, 70, 73, 117, 140, 145

Dr. Bob said that A.A.'s Twelve Steps, when simmered down to the last, quite simply resolved themselves into the words "love" and "service" (See *DR. BOB and the Good Oldtimers*, p. 338). He presented God to the old-timers as a God of love who was interested in their individual lives. (*DR. BOB, supra*, p. 110). Dr. Bob's wife, Anne, frequently quoted love verses in 1 John 4:8; 4:16–"God is love" (*DR. BOB supra*, pp. 116-17). Furthermore both Anne and her husband Dr. Bob studied Toyohiko Kagawa's book, *Love: The Law of Life.* In that book, the author Kagawa devoted an entire chapter to 1 Corinthians 13, not only to the Corinthians chapter, but also to Drummond's analysis of that chapter in Drummond's *The Greatest Thing in the World.* Hence there was much emphasis among the A.A. pioneers on the "spiritual" principle of love as it is defined in the Bible. In fact, the Big Book itself talks repeatedly of that principle of love (Big Book, 4th ed., pp. 83-84, 86, 118, 122, 153).

Love, then--the love of God--was a much cherished principle in early A.A. The AAs needed it, wanted it, studied it, and sought to know it.

Despite "higher power" divergences in current A.A. writings and meeting talk, the love of God is still a vital component of A.A. thinking and speech. Even Bill Wilson inserted the phrase "a loving God" in A.A.'s Traditions. And I well remember my good friend Seymour W., a Jew, who tried each morning to comfort his many friends in the fellowship. The telephone on Seymour's "God" line would ring for many about 6:00 A.M. The message to the bedraggled A.A. was "God loves you." And Seymour would hang up. It was a coveted privilege to be on Seymour's "God-loves-you" list. What a way to start the day in early sobriety!

Further illustrating the great store placed on God's love and on the Corinthians love principle by A.A. pioneers is their frequent rendition of Jesus Christ's message in Mark 12:30-31. These Gospel verses deal with what Jesus called the two *great* commandments:

> And thou shalt love the Lord thy God with all thy heart, and with all thy soul, and with all thy mind, and with all thy strength; this is the first commandment. And the second is like, namely this, Thou shalt love thy neighbor as thyself. There is none other commandment greater than these.

The foregoing verses, from the Gospel of Mark in the New Testament, were cited for the standard of "Absolute Love," as it was discussed in AA of Akron's *A Manual for Alcoholics Anonymous* (one of the four pamphlets commissioned by Dr. Bob for use among early AAs). The Old Testament also contained the very same commandments to which Jesus referred.

7

The Approach Early Akron A.A.'s Took While They Sought Christian Healing

Chapter Four of this title provides an explicit description exactly what the Akron "alcoholic squad"—a Christian Fellowship—did in terms of the program they followed, the elements of that program, and the description of it provided by Frank Amos to John D. Rockefeller, Jr. This present chapter will deal with the approaches they took in developing their program.

Identifying Their Alcoholism

It seems legendary that the medical profession had made little progress, if any, in curing alcoholics. And this caused more than one in that profession to declare that the "real alcoholic" was medically incurable. Varying and diverse attempts were made to describe the problem.

Popularity of the Disease Concept

Could God cure the curse of alcoholism. The Founders all said he could and would if sought, and they declared that God had cured them of the problem. Can God cure a disease? Does He say that He can and does? The pioneers knew that God could. They knew what the Bible assured them about Divine healing. They knew that God had cured the first three successful AAs. And they didn't seem to let the "disease" issue bother them.

For example, Bill Wilson credited Dr. William Duncan Silkworth, the psychiatrist who treated him at Towns Hospital in New York, with the "disease concept." According to this dictum, the alcoholic was one who had lost the ability to control his drinking. The cause, said the disease protagonists, was that he suffered from a two-fold disease: an obsession of the mind that caused him to drink and return to drinking no matter how he tried to stop and what the consequences had been. But remember that Dr. Silkworth was the one who explicitly discussed the "Great Physician" (Jesus Christ) and said that he could heal the disease.

The Obsession: To Wilson, at least, this meant that mere self-knowledge (information given and received about the life and death consequences of excessive drinking) had never produced recovery. To Wilson, it also seemed clear that fear—fear of the consequences of drinking, fear of the events occurring in one's life, and fear of the threats and cajoling of others—would not deter him from his course for very long. Moreover, Wilson seemed convinced that "will-power" was not the answer. His Big Book Chapter—More about Alcoholism—is a stroke of fine writing that points out the many things alcoholics try on their own to halt their drinking. These include solemn oaths, changes of jobs and locations, changes in the type of alcohol imbibed, and a host of other examples of attempted self-propulsion. And, when all three—self-knowledge, fear, and will-power—were brought to bear with inevitable failure, the next step was to conclude that some human resource could fill in the gap. But medicine and religion and relatives and others just had to bow out when they saw that their entreaties and threats and counseling were of no avail. This led to the final conclusion—that probably no human power could relieve one of his alcoholism.

The allergy: The stickler that eludes science and medicine to this very day is why, once the alcoholic starts drinking, he loses control over the amount he drinks. And hence, after he picks up the first drink, he drinks too much, experiences disaster, and yet returns once again. Silkworth believed this behavior was the manifestation of an allergy—a body condition that produced the phenomenon of craving once liquor was taken. I have heard all kinds of descriptions of the curse of excessive drinking ranging from genetic to nutritional to behavioral to emotional to sinful disorders; and I am not aware that anyone has yet shined the spotlight on the one or multiple causes. I do think that most of us drunks understand our problem fully. We drink. We get drunk. We encounter disaster. We return once again. I call them the Three D's and an R. I don't have an alcoholic in my family tree. I am not aware that eating was ever a problem. Nor am I sure that I drank because I was a sinner or became a sinner after I drank too much. I'm not even sure that the resultant and preceding misbehavior can be illuminated by calling it a disorder. I'd call it a disaster and leave it at that.

The Progressive Aspect: Whether the continued and increasing amount drunk, disasters encountered, and destruction caused are in the very nature of the thing, I don't know. But it doesn't take long in A.A. to realize that if you quit and then start again, things are worse than before. Having sponsored some 100 men in their recovery, I've seen them get well, get reckless, get drunk, and then go on toots that are far worse than any previous incidents reported to me. In A.A., they call these the "yets." You may not have done this or that "yet." But you will if you drink again. And I believe it.

The Spiritual Malady: I'll leave this one to some other historian or writer or to the clergy or to the theologian. Bill spelled out some ideas that, he declined to call "sins" in his later writings, amounted to "character defects" or "wrongs" or self-centered behavior that needed to be eliminated. For a time, he saw these the Oxford Group way—they were "sins" that blocked you from God. But I don't know what he saw after he eliminated the Oxford Group and the word "sin" from the A.A. vocabulary. In fact, as he himself put it, he probably did more sinning after he got sober than before, but he didn't get drunk—just disorderly!

My own view of winning the battle: The more I've read the Bible and studied the Book of James which was such an important resource to Dr. Bob, the more I see the problem in an entirely different light. First of all, I believe God can handle and cure anything. Take a look as Psalm 103 for that picture. Second, I believe what the angel told Mary: With God nothing is impossible. So what's the deal? Why do we "good" people get tangled up in so many "bad" things?

The Sin Concept

Leaving Original Sin and the "old man nature" out of the picture—and I don't really think you can—it gets down to whether we are

walking by the spirit or by the flesh. The natural man can't understand spiritual matters. The born-again Christian can ("But God hath revealed them unto us by his Spirit" See 1 Corinthians 2:7-16). But that doesn't mean that either of them is going to behave himself.

What's the problem when we don't behave? First of all, we have free will—we can choose whatever we want to do (Matthew 6:33). Second, there's a Devil out there whose primary mission, according to Jesus, is to steal and to kill and to destroy (John 10:10). Third, he's been at it endlessly and even worked over Jesus through temptations in the wilderness. Fourth, there are some Bible verses that are helpful in understanding what the Adversary does: The parable of the Sower helps to show how the Devil works (Matthew 13:1-23). The temptations the Devil offered Jesus illustrate how great is his power and how he makes it tempting (Matthew 4:1-11).

But the Devil has not awarded so many descriptive names in the Bible without their being of some use in spotting him on the prowl. Peter cautioned: "Be sober, be vigilant; because your adversary the devil, as a roaring lion, walketh about, seeking whom he may devour" (1 Peter 5:8) But the devil doesn't have so many Biblical descriptions without cause.

Thus he is called our adversary and described as a roaring, hungry lion on the prey. He is the "great dragon," the "old serpent called the devil," Satan, the "accuser" (Revelation 12, 20); "the devil that deceived them" (Revelation 10:20); and a whole lot more. He's the enemy. And Jesus called a spade a spade:

> "Why do you not understand my speech? Even because ye cannot hear my word. Ye are of your father the devil, and the lusts of your father, ye will do. He was a murder from the beginning, and abode not in the truth because there is no truth in him. When he speaketh a lie, he speaketh of his own; for he is a liar, and the father of it" (John 8:43-44).

Standing: Ephesians speaks of standing against the wiles of the devil:

> "Finally, my brethren, be strong in the Lord, and in the power of his might. Put on the whole armour of God, that ye may be able to stand against the wiles of the devil. For we wrestle not against flesh and blood, but against principalities, against powers, against the rulers of the darkness of this world, against spiritual wickedness in high places" (Ephesians 6:11-12)

In figurative form, Ephesians spells out how to "stand":

> "Wherefore take unto you the whole armour of God, that ye may be able to withstand in the evil day, and having done all, to stand. Stand therefore, having your loins girt about with truth, and having on the breastplate of righteousness; And your feet shod with the preparation of the gospel of peace. Above all, taking the shield of faith, wherewith ye shall be able to quench all the fiery darts of the wicked. And take the helmet of salvation, and the sword of the Spirit, which is the word of God; Praying always with all prayer and supplication in the Spirit, and watching thereunto with all perseverance and supplication for all saints" (Ephesians 6:13-18)

Rev. Sam Shoemaker wrote at length during the early A.A. days on Ephesians 6. See Dick B., *New Light on Alcoholism, Index*. And God offers His kids plenty of defense weapons: salvation, the renewing of the mind, Bible study, prayer, seeking guidance, fellowship with like-minded believers, the manifestations of the gift of the Holy Spirit, and lots more. He delineates some of the weapons in Ephesians 6. But all must be spiritually understood and operated by spiritual means whatever the five senses are telling us to the contrary. So that's why the Bible and revelations from God are so very important to the believer. He needs to know who the Creator is. He needs to know what the Creator does. He needs to know who God's son is and what his relationship to the Creator is. He needs to know what the Creator commands. And he needs to know how to communicate and be in fellowship with God and with His son. And then he needs to put on the whole armour of God. And stand! Not just resist. Not push! Stand—against the wiles of the devil.

This concept of overcoming the power of darkness—the power of the devil—is an important one that A.A. Akron pioneers had under their belts. The issue, for them, was not just whether they had sinned and whether their sin was drunkenness. It was to claim the redemption that Christ had accomplished which became theirs with a new birth. It was to bring in the whole armour of God that came with the redemption so that they could and would be free from guilt, condemnation, fear, and defeat. They needed to know that Jesus had come to overcome the power of the devil, and that deliverance was there for the believer.

Overcoming

So why study the Bible in A.A.? Why become a child of God in A.A.? The answer that was easiest for me to get in my head was an answer readily available to the pioneers:

> "Hereby know ye the Spirit of God: Every spirit that confesseth that Jesus Christ is come in the flesh is of God. . . . Ye are of God, little children, and have overcome them: because greater is he that is in you, than he that is in the world" (1 John 4:2, 4)

In the face of my early difficulties and the seeming impossibility of overcoming them, I just kept repeating the foregoing verse and believing it.

If you are wondering why several spinoffs from A.A. or its ideas have names like "Overcomers Outreach," "Overcomers," and "Alcoholics Victorious," you might consider the idea that they are standing on victory instead of claiming perpetual ill-health as their plight.

After you've conceded that you have free will and that you can do the things mentioned, you need to be able to recognize the devices of the Adversary and how to overcome them. The Book of James has some good suggestions: Ask for wisdom. Repudiate temptation. Be a doer of the word, not a hearer only. Follow through on your sonship by obeying the commandments. Pray for one another. Remember that the love of God and love of neighbor are the primary commandments. Know how to obey those commandments: The love of God means obeying God's commandments. The love of your neighbor means, among other things, following the precepts in 1 Corinthians 13; obeying Paul's descriptions of the don'ts and of the do's. And acquiring a solid understanding of how and what it is to become and be a child of the living and true God; how to walk by the spirit rather than by the flesh; and how to operate the manifestations of the gift of the Holy Spirit that were given to each believer "to profit withal."

Love is the first command, and it's the love of God in the renewed mind in manifestation. Obedience to God's commandments *is* the love of God, and that's not grievous, God tells us.

The Pioneer Approach

And just how would a person approach these issues? We'll see that the early A.A. pioneers took a very simple starting point:

You believe in God.

You come to Him through His son Jesus Christ.

You abstain forever.

You spurn temptation forever.

You humbly turn to the Creator for help, strength, and guidance.

You ask the Creator to take alcohol out of your life forever.

You choose to be led by the spirit of God.

You study the Word, pray, and seek guidance and get help in these endeavors. You put God's word in your mind and believe it. You study the Bible daily! You pray daily.

Then you can say that you have submitted yourself to God and that you are "resisting the devil" (James 4:7). Standing! The devil will flee, but he'll be back. And he'll be back with the same old weapons—all the sins in his suitcase, with temptation being a major assisting tool.

The pioneers had these things before them as they studied the Scriptures, prayed daily, had Quiet Times daily, fellowshipped with each other, carried out the message of what God had done for them in both love and service—reaching out by their words and deeds to fellowship with and witness to others. If you read the Book of Acts, you should be able to see a parallel between the early A.A. Christian's activities and those described in the Book of Acts. And that book describes the healings and miracles and deliverances that came to the people who believed on Jesus Christ and did these things.

8

The Practical Use and Application of This Guide

Where to Begin

If you feel lost as to where and how to begin, consider the fact that you have the whole Bible to work with. It's just a matter of deciding to focus on what the early AAs studied and how that produced their recovery ideas.

In the foregoing chapters, we have pointed to those Bible verses which were most in use. So review them. Then take the Book of James, the Sermon on the Mount, and 1 Corinthians 13, and review them. Then look at Dick B., *Why Early A.A. Succeeded*, which is a Bible study primer, and will take you through the Bible in the way the pioneers saw it.

Then there's the matter of organizing and presenting the early history. People need to have the facts about: (1) A.A.'s two different founders, two different starting points, and two kinds of ideas and practices. (2) The Akron roots, the Akron program, and the Frank Amos summary. (3) The three major offshoots from the 1939 situation when the Big Book was published. And what happened in the next 15 years that changed the whole A.A. picture. See the discussion below.

Then browse my 27 titles and decide if you want to cover Bible roots, Quiet Time, Anne Smith's Journal, Sam Shoemaker's teachings, the Oxford Group program, the literature they read, and the Christian Endeavor root. It's all there for the taking.

Consult:

The author: I'd suggest you phone or email me personally at 808 874 4876 if I can be of any help to you. Also, I'd suggest you look at four websites to see what is available and how to obtain readily that which is already up front:

My websites:

My main website is http://www.dickb.com/index.shtml; and it contains a detailed list and description of content in my historical titles.

My blog site is filled with more than 120 articles and audio talks on all phases of A.A. history: http://www.dickb-blog.com; and it is certainly a resource for familiarizing yourself with my materials and will enable you to download lots of material free.

Our AA History Bookstore, owned and managed by Terry Dunford, enables you to buy sets and individual books directly online in bulk and at discounts: http://aa-history.com/bookstore.

Our new Freedom Ranch Maui Incorporated non-profit site is designed to "teach the teachers" mainly by online outreach http://freedomranchmaui.org; and it is designed to tell you how we believe you can best carry the history message in Christian terms to the newcomer.

The purpose of this guide to help you enrich your own program with a new segment, not to burden you with just one more step guide or curriculum suggestion.

This guide is different from all Twelve Step and Christian Twelve Step guides and workbooks. It does not tell you how to "take" the Twelve Steps in any way. Nor does it tell you how to interpret or understand the Twelve Steps. Plenty of other Step guides do these things. And so does my title, *Twelve Steps for You: Take the Twelve Steps with the Big Book, A.A. History, and the Bible at Your Side.* So too does my recently published guide to accompany *New Light on Alcoholism* and to present in short form a Shoemaker approach to the Steps since he was virtually the author of them, or at least taught the ideas to Bill.

My objective has not been to add one more Step guide to the pile. My emphasis has always been on finding the Biblical sources of the Steps, organizing them, and disseminating the historical results. This Guide is can certainly be an excellent guide to using the Big Book and Twelve Steps if you choose, but in company with your learningt the distinctly different Akron program as well. Also to provide further understanding of the Biblical ideas Bill did include in the Big Book and Steps.

The Materials of others: Consult some of the many renditions and interpretations of the Steps and how to take them, if you like.

The Christian history emphasis here: But you will be filling in a huge gap in today's recovery approaches if you start here. Look on this Guide as something primarily to be used by Christians, for Christians, and with Christians or potential believers. It should also be used to show all interested parties that early A.A. was a Christian program, that AAs today have a place in A.A., and that all AAs and recovery people should seek and learn *all* of A.A.'s history—like it or not—and to seek tolerance and understanding of the views of early AAs and those AAs in A.A. today who look on the Creator, Jesus Christ, the gift of the Holy Spirit, and the Bible as a vital part of their lives and their recovery.

Decide

Once you've given some thought as to how this historical knowledge can benefit and enrich your own recovery work, it's natural to ask the question: What do I do now? In fact, I get such questions by regular and email almost every day. And the questions are yours to ask and have answered in terms of your own needs.

However, you might decide to use this guide in any of the following ways:

a) **For individual, meeting, or group use as a one-stop outline of A.A.'s Biblical roots, Christian fellowship, and original religious orientation.**

b) **As a tutorial addition to your regular treatment program, to your Christian track recovery program, or to your Christian recovery group or program.** As of the date of this writing, you certainly won't find anywhere else such a practical historical resource for Christians.

c) **Along with your own unique texts and materials.** Alcoholics Victorious, Overcomers Outreach Inc., Celebrate Recovery, and probably most of the other Christian approaches such as Teen Challenge, Alcoholics for Christ, and Youth with a Mission have written resources used with their programs. This Guide can provide an accurate historical supplement for any or all of them.

d) **To formulate a new program or curriculum or meeting that has at its base the simple desire to articulate and follow the very same and simple practices that were followed in the highly successful early A.A. program and brought cures.**

e) **To help your church, your pastor or recovery pastor, your board, your groups, and your denominations see exactly how a Christian recovery program can be undertaken in simple form and be faithful to church tenets as well.**

f) **To add a practical dimension with a scholarly source to the faith-based and faith centered communities that are proliferating—but usually proliferating out of touch with the first, effective "faith based program"—early Akron A.A.**

(g) **To provide chaplains, prison ministries, and prison evangelists with a new tool enabling them to present the A.A. and Twelve Step programs to and for Christians by emphasizing an accurate history of what early A.A. really was and how much it really accomplished.**

(h) **To have on hand in your library, in your reference materials, and on your desk this very special Christian history material.** One widely known prison ministry leader who is also a clergyman said to me some time ago: "Dick, do you know why I am providing funds for this work and obtaining your books? When I asked why, he replied, "So that I can give them to people who want to learn the real Bible history of A.A. or who disagree on the Bible's significance in the A.A. picture." Reason enough!

(i) **To buy and give free to newcomers, sponsors, counselors, therapists, chaplains, clergy, sober clubs, A.A. and other 12-Step leaders and offices, charitable agencies, health agencies, government agencies, clients, patients, and media.**

(j) **To help you select, acquire, and use these and the recommended related materials in your own recovery and life.**

Gather Resources

You probably want to ask and know just what you really need to select, acquire, and use in your own program or treatment mode. And that's an individual choice based on what you already have, where you are going, and where you have decided to go.

However, we certainly recommend the items listed here as resources.

The Bible is basic: *The Bible,* which pioneers called the "Good Book;" was the *King James Version.* You may want to use one of the so-called Twelve Step Bibles listed in our Bibliography. But there are three problems with them: (1) They won't verbalize the verses in the same language as the King James English. (2) They cover the whole Bible and parts that were not studied in early A.A. and often include comments on segments of the Bible never read by pioneers. (3) Their comments are just opinions and sometimes loaded with private Bible interpretation, psychological ideas, and therapy suggestions. You have to decide: Do I want to learn and study what early AAs studied. Or do I want a program that has been fashioned by editors and annotated with ideas of their own.

The Big Book is important: *Alcoholics Anonymous, 4th Edition*

This Guide is a must—if you want to see recovery from the viewpoint of History, the Big Book, and the Bible—as they later did and do in the Cleveland Fellowship Clarence Snyder founded.

You should have a complete set of my twenty-three historical reference titles—They can be obtained as a unit, at a discount; and they will allow you, at any time, to consult and study particular parts of the history such as Quiet Time, Anne Smith's Journal, the Oxford Group program, the literature they read, and the teachings of Rev. Sam Shoemaker that impacted so heavily on the Big Book language and Steps.

[At this writing, you can obtain the complete reference set in bulk at a major saving. Discounted to $249.95, plus $30.00 shipping and handling. From the A.A. history bookstore: http://aa-history.com/bookstore, c/o Terry Dunford, 2000 Paulele Place, Kihei, HI 96753. Prices are higher when shipped outside the United States.

Also, you can order groups of particular titles in bulk and at a discount from the bookstore so that each student or client or group member will have a copy or can be awarded a copy on an anniversary or treatment "graduation." Usually, the discount will be 50% plus shipping and handling for bulk orders of my earlier titles; and an entire box is available at $400.00 plus shipping and handling.

My later books—seven in number—plus this guide are sold by print-on-demand means; ordered by you from the bookstore; printed at once; and mailed directly to you by the printer. Since the cost is much higher for us, you will have to phone or write or email the bookstore to see if a bulk order discount of some kind can be made available to you in connection with these new 8 books.]

Early books AAs read—You may want to supplement your group study or your own reading by purchasing reprints or used copies of some of the popular early books AAs used. These would include such titles as *The Runner's Bible, The Upper Room, My Utmost for His Highest, The Meaning of Prayer, The Christ of the Mount, The Sermon on the Mount, The Greatest Thing in the World, In His Steps, Love: The Law of Life, Twice-Born Men, Varieties of Religious Experiences, For Sinners Only, Soul Surgery, Remaking the World, I Was a Pagan,* and any of Rev. Sam Shoemaker's 30 titles.

The Four AA of Akron pamphlets prepared at the behest of Dr. Bob—*A Manual for Alcoholics Anonymous, Second Reader for Alcoholics Anonymous, Spiritual Milestones in Alcoholics Anonymous,* and *A Guide to the Twelve Steps of Alcoholics Anonymous*. All are obtainable from the Akron AA Intergroup Office and perhaps from the Cleveland Intergroup Office—in bulk, at discounts, and at low, low prices.

Three A.A. "Conference Approved" titles—*DR. BOB and the Good Oldtimers; RHS* (the Grapevine Memorial issue on Dr. Bob's death); and *The Last Major Talks of the Co-founders: Biographical sketches*. The job is yours as to whether these can be purchased through regular bookstores, through Hazelden, through GSO in New York, at Intergroup or Central Offices, or at regular A.A. meetings.

The Objective

This guide is pointed exclusively at bringing deliverance to the person who still suffers. This means change! The body, the mind, and spiritual matters all require attention that results in change.

The body needs to be restored from the ravages of excessive drinking—the withdrawal pangs, the physical damage, the aches and pains and shakes, and the resultant disaster should a real alcoholic pick up just one drink.

The mind needs to be cleared of bewilderment, forgetfulness, confusion, fear, guilt, anger, dishonest thinking, focus on "more," depression, and the obsession that convinces a real alcoholic that alcohol can do no real harm and will solve anything and everything even though experience has pointed only to disaster. There's a classic saying in A.A. that very little success has been achieved if a drunken horse thief just gets sober; you still just have a sober horse thief. If the alcoholic still pursues sick thinking, he will still be sick. Worse, he'll probably yield to temptation and very possibly drink again.

The "soul" presents a different challenge. If the real alcoholic has no relationship with our Heavenly Father, he has no real defense against drunkenness save the education, will power, fear, and human resources that have not served him well. If the alcoholic is or has become a Christian, he has a relationship with Yahweh and with His son, but he can still be a carnal Christian who uses senses-knowledge and walks by the flesh instead of the spirit.

But the "sick soul" can really change and find a new and abundant life.

First, he needs salvation—a new birth in which he receives Christ and knows he has "Christ in you, the hope of glory." That's something you can handle with Romans 10:9 or through your own minister or church.

Second, he needs to understand how to walk in fellowship with the Father, His son, and other believers.

The latter walk by the spirit is the challenge of a lifetime, with the devil offering compromise, negativity, and temptation to err at every corner.

With the newcomer as the focus, the objective is to get him healed physically, mentally, and spiritually. The Creator can accomplish all these goals, but the creature has to understand and act in obedience to the will of God in order to be blessed. That, of course, is a subject Christian churches, Christian treatment, Christian recovery programs, Christian groups, and Christian literature ought to offer and probably can or do offer. And it's serious business. It doesn't need to be tabled because someone says it doesn't work, or that it is unfair to the unbeliever or the hottentot, or that it violates some supposed tradition of the fellowship.

Give the newcomer, the sponsor, the fellowship, the church and clergy, the counselor and therapist, the treatment agencies, and the non-profit and government agencies HISTORY. You can argue over treatment; you can argue over success rates; you can argue over models and methods; you can argue over theological and religious differences; and you can contest the use religious of means in any situation.

But the history is what cannot be repudiated if you learn it, understand it, and believe it. And it's Christian history. It's Bible history.

History shows conclusively that the Lord cured A.A. pioneers. It shows conclusively that they acknowledged this healing through God's power. And it shows the simple means by which they accomplished their 75 to 93% success rate.

Give people that history. Don't bury it under the guise of "separation of church and state." There is no such separation in 12 Step fellowships or in Christian approaches. "God could and would if He were sought" has been the theme of the Alcoholics Anonymous basic text in all four editions from 1939 to date. Before the publication began, it was stated even more simply by Dr. Bob: "Your Heavenly Father will never let you down!" Never!

Benefits and Diversions Arising Out of Events After 1939

Bill Wilson's frequent, severe depressions:

Bill Wilson suffered from severe depression all through his life. And it was no secret in A.A. Bill's secretary Nell Wing personally remarked to me that "the 1940's were just awful. Bill sat around just burning holes in the desk with cigarettes." Mel B. of Toledo, Ohio, has more than 54 years of sobriety. He wrote many books and articles for Hazelden and A.A. He interviewed Bill Wilson. And, Mel wrote: *My Search For Bill W.* (Center City, MN: Hazelden, 2000); and Mel, who specifically observed and researched Bill's severe depression problems, wrote:

> [**Age 10**:] It was apparently a problem that had been with him most of his life. He traced it back to age ten, when he had been tall and gawky and smaller kids could push him around in quarrels. [Bill said:] "I remember being very depressed for a year or more. .." (p. 34)

> [**Before Bill married Lois,** Bill said of Bertha Bamford, his first love, and her death:] "One morning the principal of the school came in, and at chapel he announced with a grave face that Bertha Bamford, the minister's daughter and my beloved, had died suddenly and unexpectedly the night before." [Mel B. wrote:]
> "The shock virtually wiped Bill out. He went into a deep depression, failed his courses, and also failed to graduate" (p. 115).

> [**From 1943 to 1955**:]

> [Bill wrote Lois:] "In the last twelve years of life, despite all my blessings, I have spent eight in depression, sometimes very severe ones. . . . The depressions kept me off the road and from making speeches. In fact, I was forced to sit at home and ask what would become of A.A. and what would become of me" (p. 22)

> [Mel B. wrote:] I was elated by some of Bill's statements but greatly troubled by the reference to his eight years in depression, which seemed almost a negation of the Twelve Step program. How could the A.A. program be considered at all effective if the author of the Twelve Steps couldn't find a way out of mental depression, an affliction that hits a large number of alcoholics" (p. 23)

In 1944, for example, he was invited to address the psychiatric section of the New York Medical Society. According to Lois, Bill was in a deep depression during this period and was almost incapable of performing routine activities—even going for a short walk required great effort (p. 37).

With the onset of severe depression in 1943, Bill's power drive seemed to be stalled. But since it could be quickly reactivated for important AA missions, it was still alive and well under the layer of despondency and self-doubt that plagued Bill almost regularly until 1955. . . . He also wrote *Twelve Steps and Twelve Traditions*—a book that reflects some of his depression. . . ." (pp. 38-39)

Those severe depressions seemed to have a deep effect on the way A.A. traveled and turned after Bill had published the Big Book in the Spring of 1939.

Let's take a moment and see the three new directions which seemed to be taken by AAs on their own during Bill's depression years:

(1) From mid-1939 forward, the **Akron program** began leaving the Oxford Group leaders, continued its meetings in much the same Christian Endeavor way, and found Dr. Bob working in tandem with Sister Ignatia at St. Thomas Hospital helping over 5,000 alcoholics. But Bob's wife Anne could see out of only one eye, but she couldn't see well. She was having a hard time walking, and her hands were cramped and swollen with arthritis. In 1947-48, Bill began proposing that the founders "should give the groups full control of their own affairs through establishment of a general service conference, to which the groups could send delegates. Bob had misgivings. The majority of trustees wanted no such change, nor did many of the old-timers. But in the summer of 1948, Bob learned he had cancer. And he went through much pain. On June 1, 1949, Anne Smith died. On November 16, 1950, Dr. Bob

passed away in pain. (See *DR. BOB, supra*, pp. 316-344). And from the pungent remarks of Henrietta Seiberling, Royal S., the "Orthodox Movement," and some of the old-timers, it appears the Christian Fellowship of Akron died as well (See Mitchell K. *How It Worked: The Story of Clarence H. Snyder*, 1997, pp. 207-224)

(2) From 1939, the **Cleveland program,** begun in May by Clarence Snyder, grew by leaps and bounds from one group to 30 in a year. It brought with it from Akron the Bible, the Oxford Group Four Absolutes, and the newly published Big Book and Twelve Steps. In many ways, it shined like a star that illuminated the "best" of Akron and New York and stayed afloat from the newly emerging control at GSO. It was not popular with the depressed Bill Wilson. Yet it was hailed by Bill Wilson himself as the fastest growing area in A.A. As Bill saw it, the Cleveland story as told in his book, *Alcoholics Anonymous Comes of Age.* NY: Alcoholics Anonymous World Services, 1957. The following excerpts illustrate this new, shining light:

> "Old-time Midwesterners at the Convention could remember that while all this was going on in Akron and New York, certain candles were being lighted in Cleveland which presently sent up a flame that could be seen country-wide. . . . Returning to Cleveland, they began to dig up their own prospects. . . (p. 19)

> "These multiplying and bulging meetings continued to run short of home space, and they fanned out into small halls and church basements. . . in Cleveland we saw about twenty members, not very experienced themselves, suddenly confronted by hundreds of newcomers as a result of the *Plain Dealer* Articles. How could they possibly manage? We did not know. But a year later, we *did* know; for by then Cleveland had about thirty groups and several hundred members (p. 21).

"Yes, Cleveland's results were of the best. Their results were in fact so good, and A.A.'s membership elsewhere was so small, that many a Clevelander really thought A.A. had started there in the first place" (pp. 21-22)

I believe the true impact of the Cleveland Fellowship and of Clarence Snyder's stellar role in it are yet to be appreciated. But certain major changes occurred in the thrust of A.A. in the mid-west during Wilson's depression period: (1) Cleveland embraced the original program, and more. (2) Cleveland embraced the Four Absolutes which Dr. Bob had always favored and Bill Wilson had always dodged. (3) Clarence and his friends took the Big Book and the Twelve Steps and began putting newcomers through the Steps in a day or two. "How long do you want to stay sick?" He'd say. (4) They continued the all-important hospitalization emphasis. (5) They instituted rotating leadership to assure new blood and fresh willingness. (5) Clarence wrote an epoch manual on sponsorship. (6) Clarence ultimately fathered an epoch guide to taking the Twelve Steps. (7) Clarence wrote the much needed spoof--:My higher power the lightbulb." (8) Clarence instituted spiritual retreats for AAs and their families that are still going on today in robust form.

The whole Cleveland story may never be told in full. But parts of it can be found in *DR. BOB and the Good Oldtimers*; *Alcoholics Anonymous Comes of Age*; Mitchell K., *How It Worked, supra*; Dick B., *That Amazing Grace*; and the *Legacy* guide-book mentioned just following.

People, particularly Christians already in A.A., contact me with great frequency asking how they can find—within the ranks of A.A. itself—a place where Christians feel comfortable, where the Bible is used, where prayer is involved, where fellowship is available, and where the Big Book and Twelve Steps are a vital part of the program.

My answer today is: In the Came to Believe Retreats (http://www.cametobelieve.org). Last year, three old-timer sponsees of Clarence Snyder and their wives, decided it was time to memorialize the whole show. They wanted a guidebook that reflected exactly how Clarence had taken people through the Steps in a day. They wanted it to have historical and Biblical flavor. They wanted it to show how it was done with groups at the retreats. They wanted a workbook that could actually be used by individuals and at retreats to take the Steps. They wanted additional historical resources included. And they wanted a guide as to how to organize and lead retreats of this kind. They worked for more than a year to produce what they needed. They asked me to compile and edit it. Then it was printed and made available virtually at cost. And today, thousands are in circulation and use. This resource is posted in full on several websites such as Archives International and my own blog site. And the new cametobelieve.org website sparkles with information, audio presentations, tapes and video tapes of Clarence, and information about retreat dates and places.:

The Guidebook is: *Our A.A. Legacy to the Faith Community: A Twelve-Step Guide for Those Who Want to Believe*, 2005, by Three Clarence Snyder Sponsee Old-timers and Their Wives, Compiled and Edited by Dick B. Winter Park, FL: Came to Believe Publications, 2211 Lee Road, Suite 100, Winter Park, FL 32789; 407 862-5900; steve@fbplans.com; http://www.cametobelieve.org ISBN 0-9767292-0-2.

(3) From 1939, Bill's **Big Book program** lost the impact of its developer for a decade and a half. Bill himself received the friendship and advice of Father Ed Dowling, S.J., who came to the scene in 1940 (See Robert Fiztgerald, S.J. *The Soul of Sponsorship,* but Bill himself did not seem to provide effective leadership or wide-spread inspiration and national guidance, certainly not in writings again until after Anne had died, Bob had died, and 1955 arrived with the great St. Louis Anniversary Convention. In fact, Bill had had great difficulty with Dr. Bob, with the trustees, and with old-timers selling his beloved

"Twelve Traditions" idea and power turn-over until Dr. Bob was on his deathbed.

Let's look at the proliferating and powerful substitute programs that began to come into play

(1) **In Akron**: Dr. Bob appears to have inspired four new guides to the A.A. program which were far different in form than the Big Book program; and these are still in publication today. Sister Ignatia developed two or three pamphlets that were used in her work with Dr. Bob, and she began introducing many, if not all, patients at St. Thomas to medallions and to religious ideas.

(2) **In Cleveland**: The weighty Cleveland *Central Bulletin* began publishing and included all kinds of ideas on the Bible, literature, activities, and A.A. functions. They went into sports activities. Clarence Snyder developed a method for taking newcomers through the Twelve Steps in two days, wrote the first pamphlet on sponsorship, and seems to have been responsible for establishing rotating leadership at the local level in A.A. Eventually, he fathered spiritual retreats for AAs and their families.

(3) **Elsewhere**: In these areas, I bow to the work in progress at the Hindsfoot Foundation and to the website which is growing in information and scope (http://www.hindsfoot.org). I certainly don't favor its emphasis on the 1940's and its seeming unwillingness to compare the Big Book program with the original Akron Christian Fellowship program. But it shows how much A.A. was changing in the 1940's, allegedly through four powerful outlets—all of which steered A.A. away from the original Akron program. The following represent the Hindsfoot emphasis:

> (a) *Richmond Walker* who derived from the Oxford Group—Walker's story can be found in *For*

Drunks Only, where he specifies his A.A. ideas and melds them with Oxford Group principles. In 1948, Walker wrote the *Twenty-Four Hour Book,* still in wide use especially in treatment programs. Neither could be said to embody the Akron program ideas.

(b) *Father Ralph Pfau,* a Roman Catholic Priest who wrote under the pen name John Doe and produced a large number of pamphlets that were called the *Golden Books.* The first was published in 1947. Pfau also wrote two John Doe books. All still seem to be in wide circulation and were widely read in A.A.

(c) **Edward A. Webster.** According to Hindsfoot, Webster prepared and used an "Instructor's Outline" beginning in May, 1942. In August of 1946, he published a title called The Twelve Steps, which later was published in 1949 as The Little Red Book. Coll-Webb Co. Publishers.

(d) **The Detroit Pamphlet:** In 1943, Detroit people assembled "An Interpretation of The Twelve Steps of the Alcoholics Anonymous Program." It has been called The Washington, D.C. Pamphlet, and acquired other names as used in other areas.

Let's review the modifications that peopled the period of Bill's depression but which began almost as soon as the Big Book was pubished in 1939. None was a replica of the great Akron Christian program. None was a direct follow-through on Bill's Big Book. And here they are: (1) The four Akron pamphlets published at the behest of Dr. Bob. (2) The Clarence Snyder Sponsorship pamphlet which was later followed by his guides to taking the Twelve Steps. (3) The interpretations of Richmond Walker that wound up in the Twenty Four Hour book. (4) The interpretations of Father Ralph Pfau which still have popularity among A.A.'s large Roman Catholic population. (5) The interpretations of Ed Webster ultimately embodied in The Little Red Book. (6) The interpretations of the Detroit people and their

Beginners Classes, which were laid out in the "Detroit Pamphlet" and have been copied elsewhere and revised today as "back to basics" by one interpreter who emphasizes the 1940's.

The private interpretations did not end with the 1940's. Bill engaged the help of two Roman Catholic Jesuit priests who edited his books *Twelve Steps and Twelve Traditions* and *Alcoholics Anonymous Comes of Age.*

And then came the first of several revisions of the First Edition of Alcoholics Anonymous. Piece by piece they removed the personal stories of most pioneers—stories that were largely prepared under the hand of Dr. Bob, written in Akron, and embodied their accounts of how they used the program to "find or rediscover a relationship with God."

What all this tells me is that a guide such as this one—which guides you through A.A. as it was during its peak, before Bill's depressions, and before the private interpretations of the 1940's—is and should be overdue as a welcome tool of Christians in A.A. and Twelve Step groups today.

Your Particular Program

Whether you are an individual, a group, a fellowship, a church, a religious entity, a clergyman, a therapist, a physician, a psychologist, a treatment center, a rehabilitation center, an addiction center, a research facility, or a government or non-profit agency, there's room for history in your background.

You can present it through this guidebook.

Historical Segments for Your Program: You can present it in historical segments—showing where A.A. originated (in New York and in Akron); what it took from each of its various sources; what the original program did; what its results were; precisely what the Book of James, the Sermon on the Mount in Matthew 5 to 7, and 1 Corinthians 13 contained that was considered "absolutely essential;" how to study the Bible, the elements of Christian prayer, the elements of seeking revelation from Yahweh and His son Jesus Christ; the teachings in the Bible on the Creator, the Commandments, healing and miracles, Jesus Christ, the new birth, the gift of the Holy Spirit, the remarkable Book of Acts, and the other church epistles. You can eat a whole elephant if you just take one bite at a time.

Big Book/Bible Study Groups: You can form groups and have meetings that focus on the Big Book and the Bible, Quiet Time and Meditation, the Bible and the Twelve Steps, the contents of Anne Smith's Journal, the Oxford Group life-changing program, the teachings of Rev. Samuel M. Shoemaker, the Christian literature pioneers read, the focus on United Christian Endeavor, which seemed to provide the real framework for the early program in Akron.

A.A. History Groups: These groups can focus on the origins of A.A. in Christian Endeavor and in Carl Jung's thinking; the principles and practices of the Christian Fellowship in Akron; the three outpourings of that program (the continuation of the Akron program through Sister Ignatia, the so-called "six word-of-of-mouth ideas" that Wilson said were being used; and the Big Book program.

A Biographical Study of A.A.'s transition and change in three new directions from Akron: There is a wealth of history as to just what happened in 1939 as three different programs emerged: (1) The Akron Christian program that survived until the death of Dr. Bob and Anne and the loss of Sister Ignatia. (2) The Cleveland Program, formed by Clarence Snyder in May of 1939, which embraced the Bible, the Four Absolutes, the Big Book, and the Twelve Steps and continues to this day.(3) The A.A. Fellowship structured by the Big Book and Steps. Their alteration by the four strong writings (during Bill's years of depression)—those of the Detroit Pamphlet, Ed Webster, Richmond Walker, Father Ralph Pfau, Their further alteration by the Twelve Traditions. The further alterations in the Twelve Steps and Twelve Traditions, thoroughly edited by the Jesuit Priests, Father Ed Dowling, and John Ford; and the fashioning of a Second Edition of the Big Book which began eliminating the pioneer stories and their impact.

And my favorite: The James Club. My latest title is called *The James Club and The Original A.A. Program's Absolute Essentials.* And that says it all for this guidebook. *The James Club* title contains most of the materials you would need to fill the history gap in your program. Lots of AAs with sobriety and others newer to the program are forming groups, often called The James Club Groups. I've written and posted on the internet a number of guides as to format, subjects, and content. I think you'll find lots of friends in A.A. doing this. Their work is autonomous instead of based on someone else's interpretation of the Steps, the Big Book, and the Twelve Step ideas. It often is as simple as reading James, Matthew 5 to 7, and 1 Corinthians along with other important verses. And then discussing them in and outside A.A.

Go and Tell

There are plenty of arguments today about the efficacy of Alcoholics Anonymous. Some claim the *original* Akron program was not a success. Some claim Wilson's Big Book and Steps represented a departure from the Akron ideas and were not successful by themselves. Some claim there is a need for "back to basics"—but the basics are not those of either the Akron program or the Big Book itself. All kinds of modifications have been tendered, rendered, fattened, and feathered; but the degree of their success remains unproven. Most claim that the A.A. program today is only producing a success rate of 1 to 5% though this claim brings hot denial from A.A. apologists.

After almost two decades of research, writing, and publication, we now have a pretty solid grasp of what the A.A. pioneers did, how well they fared, and how much they relied on the power of God.

I believe it is time to "Go and Tell." Not in watered down form, but in bold form that will offer truth and deliverance to those who, in increasing numbers (when the drug scene is taken into account), still need it and strongly believe: "With God nothing is impossible."

Our Creator had a great impact on A.A. in years gone by. Our Creator can have it today. Get the facts, include them in your program, and go with them!

END

Selected Bibliography

Alcohol, Science and Society: Twenty-nine Lecttures with Discussions as given at the Yale Summer School of Alcohol Studies. New Haven: Quarterly Journal of Studies on Alcohol, 1945.

Alcoholics Anonymous. New Jersey: Works Publishing Company, 1939 [the "First Edition"]

Alcoholics Anonymous, 4th ed. NY: Alcoholics Anonymous World Services, Inc., 2002.

Alcoholics Anonymous Comes of Age. NY: Alcoholics Anonymous World Services, Inc., 1957.

Alexander, William Menzies. *Demonic Possession in the New Testament: Its Historical, Medical, and Theological Aspects.* Grand Rapids: Baker Book House, 1980.

A Manual for Alcoholics Anonymous, rev. ed. AA of Akron, 1989

AA Grapevine, The: "RHS" - issue dedicated to the memory of the Co-Founder of Alcoholics Anonymous, DR. BOB. NY: The AA Grapevine, Inc., 1951.

Allen, James. *As a Man Thinketh.* NY: Peter Pauper Press, Inc., n.d.

Anderson, Bernard W. *Understanding The Old Testament.* NJ: Prentice Hall, 1957.

B., Dick. *Anne Smith's Journal, 1933-1939*, 3rd ed. Kihei, HI: Paradise Research Publications, Inc., 1998

_____. *By the Power of God: A Guide to Early A.A. Groups & Similar Groups Today.* Kihei, HI: Paradise Research Publications, Inc., 2000.

_____. *Cured!: Proven Help for Alcoholics and Addicts.* Kihei, HI: Paradise Research Publications, Inc., 2006.

_____. *Dr. Bob and His Library*, 3rd ed., Kihei, HI: Paradise Research Publications, Inc., 1998

_____. *God and Alcoholism: Our Growing Opportunity in the 21st Century.* Kihei, HI: Paradise Research Publications, Inc., 2002.

_____. *Good Morning!: Quiet Time, Morning Watch, Meditation, and Early A.A.*, 2d ed. Kihei, HI: Paradise Research Publications, Inc., 1998.

_____. *Henrietta Seiberling: Ohio's Lady with a Cause*. Kihei, HI: Paradise Research Publications, Inc., 2006.

_____. *Making Known the Biblical History and Roots of Alcoholics Anonymous*. Kihei, HI: Paradise Research Publications, Inc., 2005.

_____. *New Light on Alcoholism: God, Sam Shoemaker, and A.A.*, 2d ed. Kihei, HI: Paradise Research Publications, Inc., 1999.

_____. *The Akron Genesis of Alcoholics Anonymous*, 2d ed. Kihei, HI: Paradise Research Publications, Inc., 1998.

_____. *The Books Early AAs Read for Spiritual Growth*, 7th ed. Kihei, HI: Paradise Research Publications, Inc., 1998.

_____. *The First Nationwide A.A. History Conference*. Kihei, HI: Paradise Research Publications, Inc., 2006.

_____. *The Golden Text of A.A.: God, the Pioneers, and Real Spirituality*. Kihei, HI: Paradise Research Publications, Inc., 1999.

_____. *The Good Book and The Big Book: A.A.'s Roots in the Bible*, 2d ed. Kihei, HI: Paradise Research Publications, Inc., 1997.

_____. *The James Club and The Original A.A. Program's Absolute Essentials*, 4th ed, Kihei, HI: Paradise Research Publications, Inc., 2005

_____. *The Oxford Group and Alcoholics Anonymous*, 2d ed. Kihei, HI: Paradise Research Publications, Inc., 1998.

_____. *That Amazing Grace* (Clarence & Grace S.). Kihei, HI: Paradise Research Publications, Inc., 1996.

_____. *Turning Point: A History of Early A.A.'s Spiritual Roots and Successes*. Kihei, HI: Paradise Research Publications, Inc., 1997.

_____. *Utilizing Early A.A.'s Spiritual Roots for Recovery Today*, Rev. ed. Kihei, HI: Paradise Research Publications, Inc., 1999.

_____. *When Early AAs Were Cured and Why*, 3rd ed., Kihei, HI: Paradise Research Publications, Inc., 2006.

_____. *Why Early A.A. Succeeded: The Good Book in Alcoholics Anonymous Yesterday and Today (A Bible Study Primer)*. Kihei, HI: Paradise Research Publications, Inc., 2001.

B., Mel. *New Wine: The Spiritual Roots of the Twelve Step Miracle*. Hazelden, 1991.

_____. *Ebby: The Man Who Sponsored Bill W*. MN: Hazelden, 1998.

_____. *My Search For Bill W*. MN: Hazelden, 2000.

Barton, Bruce. *The Man Nobody Knows: A Discovery of the Real Jesus.* IN: Bobbs-Merrill, 1925.
Begbie, Harold. *Life Changers.* NY: G. P. Putnam's Sons, 1927.
_____. *Twice Born Men.* NY: Fleming H. Revell, 1909.
Best of the Grapevine, Volume II. NY: The A Grapevine, Inc., 1986.
Brown, William. *Personality and Religion.* London: University of London Press, Ltd., 1946.
Buchman, Frank N.D. *Remaking The World.* London: Blandford Press, 1961.
Bushnell, Horace. *The New Life.* London: Strahan & Co., 1868.
Cabot, Richard C. and Russell L. Dicks. *The Art of Ministering to the Sick.* NY: The Macmillan Company, 1946.
Chambers, Oswald. *My Utmost for His Highest.* Oswald Chambers Publishing Assn., 1963.
_____. *Studies in the Sermon on the Mount.* MI: Discovery House, 1960.
Clapp, Charles, Jr. *The Big Bender.* NY: Harper & Row, 1938.
Clark, Francis E. *Christian Endeavor in All Lands.* N.p.: The United Society of Christian Endeavor, 1906.
_____. *Memoirs of Many Men in Many Lands: An Autobiography.* Boston: United Society of Christian Endeavor, 1922.
Clark, Glenn. *How to Find Health Through Prayer.* NY: Harper & Row, 1940.
Cleveland Central Bulletin. Volumes I - III Cleveland Central Committee, Oct/42 - Dec/45.
Clinebell, Howard. *Understanding and Counseling Persons with Alcohol, Drug, and Behavioral Addictions.* Rev. and enl. ed. Nashville: Abingdon Press, 1998.
Comparative Study Bible. Rev ed. MI: Zondervan Publishing House, 1999.
Complete Jewish Bible. Clarksville, MD: Jewish New Testament Publications, Inc., 1998.
Daily, Starr. *Recovery.* Minnesota: Macalester Park Publishing, 1948.
_____. *Release.* NY : Harper & Brothers, 1942.
Dawson, George Gordon. *Healing: Pagan and Christian.* London: Society For Promoting Christian Knowledge, 1935.
Darrah, Mary. *Sister Ignatia.* Chicago: Loyala University Press, 1992.
Dearmer, Percy. *Body and Soul: An Enquiry into the Effects of Religion Upon Health, With a Description of Christian Works*

of Healing From the New Testament to the Present Day. London: Sir Isaac Pitman & Sons, Ltd., 1909.

DR. BOB and the Good Oldtimers. NY: Alcoholics Anonymous World Services, Inc., 1980.

Drummond, Henry. *The Greatest Thing in the World*. Fleming H. Revell, 1968.

_____. *The Ideal Life*. NY: Dodd, Mead and Company, 1898.

E., Bob. *Handwritten Note to Lois Wilson on pamphlet entitled "Four Absolutes."*

Eddy, Mary Baker. *Science and Health with Key to the Scriptures*. Boston: Published by the Trustees under the Will of Mary Baker Eddy, 1916.

Fillmore, Charles. *Christian Healing*. Kansas City: Unity School of Christianity, 1936.

Fillmore, Charles and Cora. *Teach Us to Pray*. MO: Unity School of Christianity, 1945.

Fitzgerald, Robert. *The Soul of Sponsorship: The Friendship of Fr. Dowling, S.J. and Bill Wilson in Letters*. MN: Hazelden, 1995.

Forde, Eleanor Napier. *The Guidance of God*. London: The Oxford Group, 1927.

Fosdick, Harry Emerson. *The Man from Nazareth: As His Contemporaries Saw Him*. NY: Harper & Brothers, 1949.

_____. *The Meaning of Prayer*. NY: Association Press, 1915.

Fox, Emmet. *Find and Use Your Inner Power*. NY: Harper & Brothers, 1937.

_____. *Getting Results by Prayer* (pamphlet, 1933).

_____. *Power through Constructive Thinking*. NY: Harper & Brothers, 1932.

_____. *The Sermon on the Mount*. New York: Harper & Row, 1934.

Frame, Hugh F. *Wonderful, Counsellor: A Study in the Life of Jesus*. London: Hodder And Stoughton Limited, 1935.

Frost, Evelyn. *Christian Healing: A Consideration of the Place of Spiritual Healing in the Church of To-day in the Light of the Doctrine and Practice of the Ante-Nicene Church*. London: A.R. Mobray & Co. Limited, 1940.

Gilkey, Charles Whitney. *Jesus and Our Generation*. Chicago: The University of Chicago Press, 1925.

Glover, T. R. *The Jesus of History*. New York: Association Press, 1930.

Grensted, Rev. L. W. *Psychology and God: A Study of The Implications of Recent Psychology For Religious Belief and Practice.* London: Longmans, Green and Co., 1931.
_____. *The Person Of Christ.* London: Nisbet & Co., Ltd., 1933.
Hartigan, Francis. *Bill W.*
Heard, Gerald. *A Preface to Prayer.* NY: Harper & Brothers, 1934.
Heiler, Friedrich. *Prayer: A Study in the History and Psychology of Religion.* Oxford: Oneworld Publications, 1932.
Herman, E. *Creative Prayer.* London: James Clarke & Co., Ltd., 1921.
Hickson, James Moore. *Heal The Sick.* London: Methuen & Co., 1924.
Holm, Nora Smith. *The Runner's Bible.* NY: Houghton Mifflin Company, 1913.
Inman, Philip. *Christ in the Modern Hospital.* London: Hodder & Stoughton Ltd., 1937.
James, William. *The Varieties of Religious Experience.* NY: First Vintage Press/The Library of America Edition, 1990.
New Jerusalem Bible
Jones, E. Stanley. *Christ And Human Suffering.* New York: The Abingdon Press, 1930.
_____. *The Christ of the Mount.* NY: Abingdon Press, 1930.
Jung, Carl Gustav. *Modern Man In Search of a Soul.* NY: Harcourt, Brace & World, Inc., 1933.
_____. *Psychology & Religion.* New Haven: Yale University Press, 1938.
_____. *The Psychogenesis of Mental Disease.* NY: Bolingen Foundation, 1960.
K., Mitchell. *How It Works.* NY: Big Book Study Group, 1999.
K., Richard. *New Freedom: Reclaiming Alcoholics Anonymous,* Haverhill, MA: 2005.
_____. *So You Think Drunks Can't Be Cured.* Haverhill, MA: 2003
_____. *Separating Fact From Fiction.* Haverhill, MA: 2003.
Kagawa, Toyohiko. *Love: The Law of Life.* Philadelphia: The John C. Winston Company, 1929.
Kelsey, Morton T. *Psychology, Medicine & Christian Healing.* Rev. ed. San Francisco: Harper & Row, Publishers, 1966.
Kenyon, E. W. *Jesus the Healer.* Kenyon's Gospel Publishing Society, Inc., 2000.
_____. *The Wonderful Name of Jesus.* Kenyon's Gospel Publishing Society, 1998.

King James Version, Authorized
Kitchen, V. C. *I Was a Pagan*. NY: Harper & Brothers, 1934.
Kurtz, Ernest. *Not-God: A History of Alcoholics Anonymous*, Exp ed. Hazelden, 1991.
Laubach, Frank. *Prayer (Mightiest Force in the World)*. NY: Fleming H. Revell, 1946.
Laymon, Charles M. *A Primer of Prayer*. Nashville: Tidings, 1949.
Lean, Garth. *On The Tale of a Comet*. CO: Helmers & Howard, 1988.
Lewis, C. S. *Miracles: How God Intervenes in Nature and Human Affairs*. NY: Collier Books, 1960.
Lois Remembers. NY: Al-Anon Family Group Hqs., 1979.
Lupton, Dilworth. *Religion Says You Can*. Boston: The Beacon Press, 1938.
Macmillan, Ebenezer. *Seeking and Finding*. NY: Harper & Brothers, 1933.
Maillard, John. *Healing in the Name of Jesus*. London: Hodder & Stoughton, 1936.
Markey, Morris. *Alcoholics and God*. Liberty Magazine, 1939.
McCarthy, Katherine. *The Emmanuel Movement and Richard Peabody* (Journal of Studies on Alcohol, Vol. 45, No. 1, 1984).
Micklem, E. R. *Miracles & The New Psychology: A Study in the Healing Miracles of the New Testament*. London: Oxford University Press, 1922.
Mitchel, Dale. *Silkworth: The Little Doctor Who Loved Drunks*. Center City, MN: Hazelden, 2002.
Moody, Dwight L. *Secret Power: Or, The Secret of Success in Christian Life and Work*. Chicago: F. H. Revell, 1881.
Mosely, Rufus. *Perfect Everything*. MN: Macalester Park Publishing, 1949.
Murch, James DeForest. *Successful C.E. Prayer-Meetings*. OH: Standard Publishing Co., 1930.
New Bible Dictionary, Second Edition. England: Inter-Varsity Press, 1982.
Newton, James Draper. *Uncommon Friends*. NY: Harcourt Brace, 1987.
Our A.A. Legacy to the Faith Community: A Twelve-Step Guide for Those Who Want to Believe. By Three Clarence Snyder

Sponsee Old-timers and Their Wives. Compiled and Edited by Dick B., Winter Park FL: Came to Believe Pubications, 2005.

P. Wally. *But for the Grace of God.* WV: The Bishop of Books, 1995.

Parker, William R. and Elaine St. Johns. *Prayer Can Change Your Life.* New ed. NY: Prentice Hall, 1957.

Pass It On. NY: *Alcoholics Anonymous World Services*, 1984.

Peabody, Richard R. *The Common Sense of Drinking.* Atlantic Monthly Press Book, 1939.

Peale, Norman Vincent. *The Positive Power of Jesus Christ.* NY: Foundation for Christian Living, 1980

_____. *The Power of Positive Thinking.* NY: Peale Center for Christian Living, 1978.

Peele, Stanton. *Diseasing of America.* San Francisco: Jossey Bass Publishers, 1995.

Pittman, Bill. *AA The Way It Began.* Seattle: Glen Abbey Books, 1988.

Pittman, Bill and B., Dick. *Courage to Change: The Christian Roots of the Twelve-Step Movement.* MN: Hazelden.

Pridie, J. R. *The Church's Ministry of Healing.* London: Society For Promoting Christian Knowledge, 1926.

Puller, F. W. *The Anointing of the Sick in Scripture and Tradition, with some Considerations on the Numbering of the Sacraments.* London: Society For Promoting Christian Knowledge, 1904.

Rawson, F. L. *The Nature of True Prayer.* England: The Society for Spreading The Knowledge of True Prayer, 1918.

Recovery Devotional Bible: New International Version. Grand Rapids, MI: Zondervan Publishing House, 1993.

Redwood, Hugh. *God in the Shadows.* London: Hodder & Stoughton, 1934.

Richardson, Alan. *The Miracle-Stories of the Gospels.* London: SCM Press Ltd, 1941.

Rotherham's Emphasized Bible. MI: Kegel Publications, 1994.

Schaer, Hans. *Religion and The Cure of Souls in Jung's Psychology.* NY: Bolingen Foundation, 1950.

Schaff, Philip. *History of the Christian Church, Volume I*, 3rd Revision (Grand Rapids., MI: Wm B. Eerdman's Publishing Company, 1890.

Second Reader for Alcoholics Anonymous. Akron: AA of Akron, n.d.

Serenity: A Companion for Twelve Step Recovery. Nashville: Thomas Nelson Publishers, 1990.

Shafto, G. R.H. *The Wonders of the Kingdom: A Study of the Miracles of Jesus*. NY: George H. Doran Company, 1924.

Shoemaker, Samuel M., Jr. *Children of the Second Birth*. NY: Fleming H. Revell, 1927.

_____. *Confident Faith*. NY: Fleming H. Revell, 1932.

_____. "How to Find God." *The Calvary Evangel*, July, 1957.

_____. *Realizing Religion*. NY: Association Press, 1923.

_____. *Religion That Works*. NY: Fleming H. Revell, 1928.

_____. *The Experiment of Faith*. NY: Harper & Brothers, 1957.

_____. *The Gospel According to You*. NY: Fleming H. Revell, 1934.

_____. *Twice-Born Ministers*. NY: Fleming H. Revell, 1929.

Smith, Bob and Sue Smith Windows. *Children of the Healer*. IL: Parkside Publishing, 1992.

Speer, Robert E. *Studies of the Man Christ Jesus*. NY: Fleming H. Revell, 1896.

_____, *The Principles of Jesus*. NY: Fleming H. Revell, 1902.

Spiritual Milestones in Alcoholics Anonymous. Akron: AA of Akron, n.d.

Stafford, Tim. "The Hidden Gospel of the 12 Steps." *Christianity Today*, July 22, 1991.

Stalker, James. *The Life of Jesus Christ*. NY: Fleming H. Revell, 1891.

Streeter, B. H. *The God Who Speaks*. London: Macmillan & Co., Ltd., 1936.

Streeter, B. H. (Editor). *The Spirit: God and His Relation to Man Considered From The Standpoint of Philosophy, Psychology And Art*. London: Macmillan And Co., 1919.

Taylor, Vincent. *The Formation of the Gospel Tradition: Eight Lectures*. London: Macmillan & Co. Ltd., 1964.

Temple, William. *Christus Veritas: An Essay*. London: Macmillan & Co Ltd., 1954.

The Book of Yahweh, 7th ed.. Abilene, TX: The Houses of Yahweh, 1994.

The Co-founders of Alcoholics Anonymous: Biographical sketches Their last major talks, 1972, 1975.

The Complete Parallel Bible. Oxford: Oxford University Press, 1993.

The Contemporary Parallel New Testament (Eight Translations). NY: Oxford University Press, 1997.

The Dead Sea Scrolls Bible. HarperSanFrancisco, 1999.
The Life Recovery Bible: The Living Bible. Wheaton, IL: Tyndale House Publishers, 1992.
The Revised English Bible, New Testament.
The Schocken Bible: Volume I (The Five Books of Moses). NY: Schocken Books, 1995.
The Tidings. March 24, 1943.
The Upper Room (Methodist quarterly periodical which began publishing in April, 1935).
Tileston, Mary Wilder. *Daily Strength for Daily Needs.*
Tournier, Paul. *The Healing of Persons.* NY: Harper & Row, Publishers, 1965.
_____. *The Person Reborn.* NY: Harper & Row, Publishers, 1966.
Troward, Thomas. *The Edinburgh Lectures on Mental Science.* NY: Dodd, Mead & Co., 1909.
Vine's Expository Dictionary of Old and New Testament Words.
Walker, Richmond. *For Drunks Only.* Center City, MN: Hazelden., n.d.
Weatherhead, Leslie D. *Psychology and Life.* New York: Abingdon Press, 1935.
_____. *Psychology, Religion, and Healing.* NY: Abingdon-Cokesbury Press, 1951.
Wells, Amos R. *Expert Endeavor: A Text-book of Christian Endeavor Methods and Principles.* Boston: United Society of Christian Endeavor, 1911.
White, William L. *Slaying the Dragon: The History of Addiction Treatment and Recovery in America.* Bloomington, IL: Chestnut Health Systems/Lighthouse Institute, 1998.
Willitts, Ethel R. *Healing in Jesus Name.* Crawfordsville, IN: Ethel R. Willitts, Publisher, 1931.
Wilson, Jim. *Healing Through The Power of Christ.* London: James Clarke & Co., Ltd., 1946.
Wilson, W. G. *Bill W.: My First 40 Years.* Center City, MN: Hazelden, 2000.
_____. *W. G. Wilson Reflections.* Bedford Hills, NY: Stepping Stones Archives, 1954.
Wing, Nell. *Grateful to Have Been There.* IL: Parkside Publishing Corporation, 1992.
Worcester, Elwood and Samuel McComb. *The Christian Religion as a Healing Power.* NY: Moffat, Yard And Company, 1909.

Worcester, Elwood and Samuel McComb, Isador H. Coriat. *Religion and Medicine: The Moral Control of Nervous Disorders.* New York: Moffat, Yard & Company, 1908.

Young's Analytical Concordance. Grand Rapids, MI: Robert Young, n.d.

Appendix One

Catch the Wave

There are a number of things I didn't hear in my secular treatment center program. Nor did I hear much of them in A.A. Yet they have much to do with successful recovery by a born-again Christian. They may also be something that needs to be included in your particular program lest your wave roll onto the shore without your riding on the crest.

AAs frequently say something like: "We are not bad people trying to be good. We are sick people trying to get well." Or, "All we have is today." Or, "My best thinking got me here." Or, "Don't think, don't drink, just go to meetings." Or, "I don't know whether this is self-will or God's will." Or, "I ask my Higher Power what to do." Or, "Just don't drink and go to meetings." Or, "I was just a liar, a cheat, and a thief." "All I have is a daily reprieve. . ." Or, "I'm in a relationship, and it's kicking my butt." Or, "My committee [the thoughts in my head] has been acting up." Or, "What I really need is a meeting." Or, "I need to get to a meeting and dump!" Or, "Thank goodness, A.A. is spiritual, but not religious." Or, "If you mention God, you'll drive newcomers out of the rooms."

Any devoted AA can verify these and add dozens more that he or she has heard in the rooms. And I've heard some older ones add: "Is this all there is?"

The answer is: It certainly doesn't have to be. Nor do you need to leave A.A. to find the real deal. But the real deal will never sound like the sick, negative, guilt-ridden, mentally confused, despairing, fatalistic secular observations that are commonplace in meetings devoid of mention of the Bible, of the Creator, of Jesus Christ, or the revelations received through manifesting the gift of the Holy Spirit.

For a long time, the most sane remarks I heard in early sobriety came from a group of elderly gents (like myself) who were frequenting my treatment center's after-care men's group. I was the one who was shaking, frightened, depressed, confused, and negative yet fighting to believe things would get better. Some of the old birds would tell jokes. Some would talk about their families. Some would say: "Alcoholics can have fun, Dick." Some would tell me: "It's going to get better." But not a one ever said that God could help. Not a one mentioned the Bible. Not a one mentioned Jesus Christ. Rarely did anyone mention prayer—and even then, only in some general term. And only one that I can think of was ever out in the trenches looking for new people to help. They all liked the comfort of our gentleman's club. And so did I. But they didn't do anything significant in A.A. Most attended a paid-for men's group with a counselor. None ever showed up at dances, conferences, retreats, seminars, or service functions. None sponsored anyone.

Before long, I was in the V.A. Psych Ward stone, cold, sober. Shaking with anxiety and filled with despair. Clinging to A.A. by taking the nuts out to A.A. meetings with me in San Francisco in the evenings. And but for that slim rope, I seemed to have little to hang onto.

The rest of the story is about reading the Bible, prayer, attending a Bible fellowship on weekends, spending more time with believers, and listening to tapes. It's also about very soon going to court without fear, going to prison without fear, looking at the newspaper without fear, and doing my best to stand on the promises of God.

All the foregoing didn't really lead me to catching my wave. Not for a while. I had become a child of God and received the gift of the Holy Spirit rather soon after I returned from a trip to the Holy Land in 1979. But I continued to drink and thought very little about loving and serving and fellowshipping with my Heavenly Father and His kids even though I was wrapped up in finding all about the sources of the Bible.

It took the final disaster to get me ready to ride the wave of deliverance. And what a ride it was to be.

The First Step: What Does our Heavenly Father Say?

Some powerful Bible verses clued me in:

"Trust in the LORD with all thine heart; and lean not unto thine own understanding. In all thy ways acknowledge him, and he shall direct thy "paths" (Proverbs 3:5-6)

"I waited patiently for the LORD and he inclined unto me, and heard my cry. He brought be up also out of an horrible pit, out of the miry clay, and set my feet upon a rock, and established my goings" (Psalm 40:1-2)

"The thief cometh not, but for to steal, and to kill, and to destroy: I am come that they might have life, and that they might have it more abundantly" (John 10:10).

"Beloved, I wish above all things that thou mayest prosper and be in health, even as thy soul prospereth" (3 John 2)

"But whoso keepeth his word, in him verily is the love of God perfected: hereby we know that we are in him. He that saith he abideth in him ought himself so to walk, even as he walked" (1 John 2:5-6)

"My little children, let us not love in word, neither in tongue; but in deed and in truth. And hereby we know that we are of the truth, and shall assure our hearts before him. For if our heart condemn us, God is greater than our heart, and knoweth all things. Beloved, if our heart condemn us not, then we have confidence toward God. And whatsoever we ask, we receive of him, because we keep his commandments, and do those things that are pleasing in his sight. And this is his commandment, That we should believe on the name of his Son Jesus Christ, and love one another, as he gave us commandment" (1 John 3:18-23).

"Ye are of God, little children, and have overcome them: because greater is he that is in you, than he that is in the world" (1 John 4:4)

"Beloved, let us love one another: for love is of God; and every one that loveth is born of God, and knoweth God. He that loveth not knoweth not God; for God is love" (1 John 4:7-8).

"There is no fear in love; but perfect love casteth out fear: because fear hath torment, He that feareth is not made perfect in love" (1 John 4:18).

"For God hath not given us the spirit of fear; but of power, and of love, and of a sound mind" (2 Timothy 1:7)

"If ye then be risen with Christ, seek those things which are above, where Christ sitteth on the right hand of God. Set your affection on things above, not on things of the earth" (Colossians 3:1-2)

"Let the word of Christ dwell in you richly in all wisdom, teaching and admonishing one another in psalms and hymns and spiritual songs, singing with grace in your hearts to the Lord. And whatsoever ye do in word or deed, do all in the name of the Lord Jesus, giving thanks to God and the Father by him" (Colossians 3:16-17).

"And be not conformed to this world: but be ye transformed by the renewing of your mind, that ye may prove what is that good, and acceptable, and perfect, will of God" (Romans 12:2).

"Who shall separate us from the love of Christ? Shall tribulation, or distress, or persecution, or famine, or nakedness, or peril, or sword. . . . Nay, in all these things we are more than conquerors through him that loved us. For I am persuaded, that neither death, nor life, nor angels, nor principalities, nor powers, nor things present, nor things to come. Nor height, nor depth, nor any other creature shall be able to separate us from the love of God, which is in Christ Jesus our Lord" Romans 8:35, 37-39).

"And God is able to make all grace abound toward you; that ye, always having all sufficiency in all things, may abound to every good work" (2 Corinthians 9:8)

"Now unto him that is able to do exceeding abundantly above all that we ask or think, according to the power that worketh in us" (Ephesians 3:20).

"And Jesus answered him, The first of all the commandments is, Hear, O Isreael: The Lord our God is one Lord. And thou salt love the Lord thy God with all thy heart, and with all thy soul, and with all thy mind, and with all thy strength: this is the first commandment. And the second is like, namely this, Thou shalt love thy neighbor as thyself. There is none other commandment greater than these" (Mark 12:29-31)

"And these signs shall follow them that believe; In my name shall they cast out devils; they shall speak with new tongues; They shall take up serpents; and if they drink any deadly thing, it shall not hurt them; they shall lay hands on the sick, and they shall recover" (Mark 16:17-18).

"And whatsoever ye do, do it heartily, as to the Lord, and unto men" (Colossians 3:23).

"See that none render evil for evil unto any men; but ever follow that which is good, both among yourselves, and in all men. Rejoice evermore. Pray without ceasing. In every thing give thanks: for this is the will of God in Christ Jesus concerning you" 1 Thessalonians 5:15-18)

The Second Step: To Be a Doer of the Word

About the Good Book—the "Word of God": Romans 12:1-2 tell us how much our walk by the spirit of God depends on our renewing our minds to what the Word of God says about our Father, about what Jesus Christ accomplished and made available to us, and about our power to act in the name of Jesus Christ. We can "prove" what the will of God is when we become convinced to the point of action that what it says is true, then controlling what goes in our mind as to what God says is the truth, and then walking out on what He says, believing that He makes good on His promises.

> Think what the Word says, not what the world says. [If you "think" you are an alcoholic and cannot be cured by the power of God, then you are not thinking what the Word says: "By his stripes ye were healed."]

> Say what the Word says, not what the world says. [If you keep confessing negatives about fear, sickness, and a lurking urge and allergy, then you are not saying what

the Word says: "For God hath not given us the spirit of fear, but of power and of love and of a sound mind."]

Do what the Word says, not what the world does. [If you walk like a cripple and act like a cripple, then you are not acting in accord with what the Word says: "Who healeth all our diseases"]

If any of you lack wisdom, ask of God who gives to all men liberally. [If you wonder what to do, worry about what to do, and are confused about what to do, then you are letting your mind contradict what the Word says: "I can do all things through Christ which strengtheneth me;" and "God is not the author of confusion"]

The Third Step: Praise, Be Thankful, and Enjoy

Trust God, don't drink, and:

Get together with believers and do your thing with them—exercise; go to sports events, movies, restaurants, athletic events, dances, camp-outs, retreats, hikes, conferences, meetings, sober clubs, ski trips, fishing, card games, shows, races, amusement parks.

And crest the wave in Maui, Hawaii, by

Going to the beach, surfing, wind-surfing, driving to the top of Haleakala Crater, bicycling down from the Crater, snorkeling, scuba diving, big sea fishing, sailing, whale-watching, turtle riding, golfing, playing tennis, riding horseback, traveling round the Islands on a cruise ship, enjoying a luau, paddling a kayak, taking a helicopter ride over the Crater or down to Hana or into the Iao Gorges, getting married on the beach, seeing the rainbows, seeing the flowering trees, seeing the Poinsettia in bloom, seeing the Protea in bloom, seeing the tropical plants and gardens, seeing the cane fields, seeing the pineapple fields, seeing the orchids, seeing the Iao Needle, barbecuing at the beach parks, jogging, swimming, swrimming under the waterfalls, taking in the scenic views, listening to Hawaiian music, seeing the Jacaranda trees in bloom, lunching at the Kula Lodge, visiting the hotel complexes and golf courses at Wailea, Kanapaali, and Kapalua, taking a boat trip to Lanai and Molokai, seeing the flying fish and porpoises on the way, bubbling in the outdoor spa, getting a tan, conking out on the beach, swimming in the ocean, strolling along the road, and buying a condo or a time share.

In fact, come to Maui and heal!

Keep Your Love Light Shining

With lots of laughter, smiles, hugs, pats, I love you's, thank you's, encouraging words, naming your blessings, praying for those in need, and helping others.

Sing! The Oxford Group people sang. Churches sing. Bible fellowships sing. Beach parties sing. Sing-along the way in A.A.—why don't we?

Put Your Heavenly Father First

Cultivate the habit of prayer. Read the Bible daily. Ask our Heavenly Father what He would have you do, where He would have you go, how He would have you serve, and what you can do to glorify Him and His son Jesus Christ. Give praise. Give thanks. Rejoice. "This is the day which the Lord hath made. Rejoice and be glad in it."

Take Care of Yourself

Keep yourself in shape: Vitamins, minerals, supplements, weights, exercise 30 minutes a day, do breathing exercises, seek regular dental care, nutritious foods, lots of fiber and water with plenty of green tea, blueberries, and wild salmon! Even dark chocolate now!

Eliminate the Stress

Fill your hours with family, job, hobbies. recreation, education, reading, TV, volunteer work, religious activities, church, stretches, exercise, and plenty of communication and fellowship with others. Get a pet. Take time out for breathers.

Stop thinking negatives. Stop talking about negatives. Stop acting on negatives. Think and act: "I am a son of God with all power."

See the Doctor Regularly

That's not all there is, but it sure beats the old ways, old crowds, old disasters, and old miseries.

And You Have Christ in You, the Hope of Glory!

When Jesus Christ returns, you'll be with Him – forever and ever!

END

Do we really need to suggest all this as part of adding Christian Fellowship history to your program? I believe we do. Thus, when Dr. Bob was asked a question about the program, he's say: "What does the Good Book say? He wasn't reflecting negative thoughts and deeds. Dr. Bob enjoyed his wife and family, playing bridge, fishing, driving a flashy car, going to retreats, reading, praying, studying the Bible, helping others to get well, passing along good books, and looking to His Heavenly Father for the answers—then "going about his Father's business." When Anne was asked for counsel or advice, she's ask if the person had observed a Quiet Time. Then she'd quote a relevant verse; and if she couldn't think of one, she'd simply quote 1 John 4:8: "God is love." Keep that one in your mind. That'll do.

Appendix Two

A.A. History Study Meetings

You may want to call yours "The James Club" or "The Big Book/Bible Study Group"

Studying the History, Bible Roots, Big Book, and Twelve Steps

How you and your A.A. and 12-Step friends can meet freely to study, learn, compare, and discuss our basic roots and text

---

Abstract

This is for individuals who believe in, want to investigate, or wish to learn and understand the basic Bible verses and Biblical ideas studied by A.A. pioneers. And compare and contrast them with the teachings of A.A.'s mentors and with the basic ideas and principles that were incorporated into A.A.'s Big Book and Twelve Steps. Many AAs and 12-Step groups have written me asking where and how they can begin "Big Book/Bible Study" meetings and groups. Here we tell you where such seekers—if they want to follow the footsteps of our founders—should focus and read as a group in the Bible and the Big Book. We suggest reviewing the sources that propelled the basics into the A.A. Fellowship. We give you specific places read, which we believe which will help every member, leader, facilitator, group, speaker, or student. We show what the founders read and did and what you can do to understand better the of "spiritual" recovery program in the Big Book and Twelve Steps. If you are asking about recovery and cure, use this guide. Discover right now where you should start, what you what you should read, and how you and your friends or group will benefit by learning the specific resources adopted and used in pioneer A.A.

Parts of the Good Book A.A. Old-Timers Considered "Absolutely Essential"

"Dr. Bob, noting that there were no Twelve Steps at the time and that 'our stories didn't amount to anything to speak of,' later said they were convinced that the answer to their problems was in the Good Book. 'To some of us older ones, the parts that we found absolutely essential were the Sermon on the Mount, the 13th chapter of First Corinthians, and the Book of James,' he said." See *DR.BOB and the Good Oldtimers.* NY: Alcoholics Anonymous World Services, Inc., 1980, p. 96.

[Dr. Bob addressed the subject this way:] "Members of Alcoholics Anonymous begin the day with a prayer for strength and a short period of Bible reading. They find the basic messages they need in the Sermon on the Mount, in Corinthians and the Book of James" (quoted in an Akron, Ohio, A.A. pamphlet of the 1940's—published by the Friday Forum Luncheon Club of the Akron A.A. Groups; and see Dick B. *Cured.* HI: Paradise Research Publications, Inc., 2006, p. 4)

Why this Guide is Needed

In the last sixteen years, A.A. members—and a great many recovery groups—have shown a long overdue and certainly promising interest in early A.A.'s beginnings. They seem to understand that a rapidly changing and diversifying fellowship needs to keep its origins in mind.

The trend can easily be recognized in the growing number of books, articles, websites, forums, conferences, and groups which have made 12-Step history a sole or major priority.

But the new historical zeitgeist has yet to reach and motivate recovery professionals, 12-Step groups or individuals, or their meetings to a flourishing application to the spiritual program that marked early A.A. cures.

The following are among the reasons for the obvious hole and lack of information: (1) Unfamiliarity with, or lack of access to, informative, accurate, comprehensive historical materials. (2) Preoccupation with this or that dynamic that promotes a particular medical, psychological, religious, therapeutic, treatment or rehab program approach. (3) Prejudice against mention of religious matters above a whisper. (4) Inordinate concern over who, what ideas, and what literature should be excluded from recovery talk and meetings. (5) A present and recognizable tendency to place universalism, "treatment," stereotyped practices, and profitable book sales above those things which originally produced such remarkable cures among seemingly helpless and hopeless, "medically incurable" alcoholics and addicts. (6) A zeal for medical, psychological, and government grants that pushes to the side the primary purpose of A.A. to reach out to, and help newcomers. (7) Absence of informed, effective teachers and facilitators. (8) A tendency to argue about, and suppress any writing or talk that conflicts with present-day views. Phrased differently, claiming that history, God, and religion endanger the "simple" detritus being hurled into the scene today—replacing tried and true early A.A. components such as the Bible, Christian literature, the teachings of Rev. Sam Shoemaker, Oxford Group literature and principles (9) Outright rejection of the historically significant observations journal of Anne Ripley Smith, Dr. Bob's wife, accompanied by omission of pioneer emphasis on Quiet Time with its Bible study, prayers, seeking of guidance, use of devotionals, and religious literature that enhanced an understanding of the "spiritual."

I have received thousands of communications by letter, phone, fax, and email from people wanting to know where and how to begin and continue their education about our history, the Bible, and the relationship of each to the program as it exists today. The writers almost as often ask about the success rates (75% to 93%) in early A.A. and the success rate in today's A.A. (1% to 5%). Most inquirers lack an effective guide—usually none at all. Many lack a solid cadre for group study. Most can find no willing leadership. Almost all forget that early A.A. and just about every continuing A.A. group today sprang from very humble beginnings—involving as few as two or three members in search of relief from the curse of alcoholism. People who were not experts, who were not afraid to learn from medicine and religion, who sought God's help, and abstained from liquor and temptation while relief was on the way.

On the other hand, those of us in direct touch with religious, medical, and scholarly inquisitors, as well as thousands of still-suffering alcoholics and addicts, know that there is a loud thundering today for facts. Facts about early A.A., its roots, and its astonishing pioneer success rate. Facts explaining what the pioneers meant when they said they were cured. Facts explaining how and whether individual religious convictions can be squared with an ever-growing secular trend and secularist intrusions into the recovery groups as well.

This capsule will briefly present tools, sources of tools, experiences, hindrances, and specific ideas about how to organize a study meeting or group, how to conduct its meetings, how to use resources that will form the basis for education and instruction, and how a leader, facilitator, chairperson, or individual can move out at once.

Begin with the Bible Itself

I can offer no better place to begin than with the Good Book itself. Dr. Bob's wife wrote in the journal she shared with early AAs:

> Of course the Bible ought to be the main Source Book of all. No day ought to pass without reading it (See Dick B., *Anne Smith's Journal, 1933-1939*, 3rd ed. HI: Paradise Research Publications, Inc., 1998, p. 82).

Dr. Bob said that old timers believed the answer to their problems was in the Bible, which he and they called the Good Book. He also stated emphatically that A.A. took its basic ideas from their study and effort in the Bible.

From the outset keep your objectives simple.

Begin where the pioneers began. Begin where both Dr. Bob and Anne began. Make sure your studies will be grounded on the Bible. Obtain a copy of the *King James Version* of the Bible. Bring it to the meeting, and keep it in front of you and in front of every person studying with you. This means, of course, that every student should own and bring, or be provided by your group with, the Bible. Don't leave home without it!

Stick with the *King James Version*, whatever your preference, because *King James* is what the pioneers used. You will relate better to their thinking and practice if you use it.

Previously we have quoted: Dr. Bob's statements that three parts of the Bible were considered "absolutely essential" in the early program—the Book of James, the Sermon on the Mount (Matthew 5 to 7), and 1 Corinthians 13. Anne Smith read to Dr. Bob and Bill every day in the summer of 1935.

Bill Wilson pointed out that Anne frequently read from the Book of James, which Bill said was "our favorite." So your first study should be in the Book of James

James

As Bill Wilson himself said: Anne Smith read to Dr. Bob and Bill every day in the summer of 1935 when Bill was living with the Smiths in Akron. She frequently read from the Book of James, which Bill said was "our favorite."

Snippets from James can still easily be spotted in the Big Book. For example: (1) "Father of lights" (James 1:17). (2) "Thou shalt love thy neighbor as thyself" (James 2:8). (3) "Faith without works is dead" (James 2:20). (4) And the "confess your faults" language in James 5:16.

Therefore, we strongly suggest that you start your meetings in the Book of James. It is simple, easy to understand, and a clear mirror of what the pioneers saw in the Bible.

First, pursue all chapters and every verse in the Book of James. Spend more than one meeting on this book if you wish. Follow our suggestions; and you can later apply those suggestions to your studies of the Sermon on the Mount and 1 Corinthians 13

As we wrote, Anne Smith read to Dr. Bob and Bill every day in the summer of 1935. She frequently read from the Book of James, which Bill said was "our favorite." *DR. BOB and the Good Oldtimers* reports the following thoughts and remarks of Bill:

> "For the next three months, I lived with these two wonderful people," Bill said. "I shall always believe they gave me more than I ever brought them." Each morning, there was a devotion, he recalled. After a long silence, in which they awaited inspiration and guidance, Anne would read from the Bible. "James was our favorite," he said, "Reading from her chair in the corner, she would softly conclude, 'Faith without works is dead'," This was a favorite quotation of Anne's, much as the Book of James was a favorite with early A.A.'s—so much so that "The James Club" was favored by some as a name for the Fellowship." (See *DR. BOB*, *supra*, p.71).

Second, study all the verses in the Book of James

I've usually suggested to men I sponsor that the way to eat an elephant is one bite at a time. Don't try to read the entire Bible before beginning. Don't even focus on the Gospels, Acts, or the church epistles. Just one chunk of reading at a time.

Open every meeting with prayer and ask all present to pray specifically that God guide and bless the reading and illuminate your understanding of it.

Take your Bibles. Open them to the Book of James. Don't start until everyone has found the correct page. Appoint one person to read the Book of James out loud while others silently read along in their Bibles as the speaker reads it aloud.

Eyes on the page! Don't try to read all the chapters of James at one session unless the flow is smooth and within your time limits. No questions. No teaching. No discussion. Just a reading of the Book of James. your leader should read aloud, all or as much as you like, of the Book of James. Others silently read along with the speaker.

Before proceeding further, you and your leader might want to read the same material more than once. Don't hesitate to do just that.

[Note: When you have completed all segments of your study of James, including the instructions in the following paragraphs, you are then ready and able to do the same thing with the Sermon on the Mount, and then with 1 Corinthians 13].

Here we continue with your instructions as to James.

Third, study the part of my title *The James Club and The Original A.A. Program's Absolute Essentials* that reviews and explains the verses in James you have just read. Compare each relevant segment in my title with the part or parts you have just read in James.

I have reviewed the Book of James, verse by verse, thoroughly in several of my titles. But I believe the best and most recent analysis is in my title *The James Club and The Original A.A. Program's Absolute Essentials* (Kihei, HI: Paradise Research Publications, 2006). Your greatest benefit will come if each student has a copy of that resource.

Appoint one person to read the explanatory resource out loud just as was done with the Bible itself. To begin, turn to pages 51-52 of my title *When Early AAs Were Cured and Why--or preferably to the appropriate pages in my title The James Club, supra..* At the first James session, your leader should read my commentary aloud, beginning at page 51 of *When Early AAs*.... He or she should continue reading until he or she has read as much of the relevant commentary as deals with what the leader covered in the reading from James. Other students should silently follow the reading in their own copy of the resource. No questions. No teaching. No discussion. Not yet!

The reason for keeping audience silence during any reading by the leader is that questions and discussion often divert attention from the speaker, from the content being read, and from the audience's concentration on the intended focus. Also, answers and explanations may often come in the very next sentence or chapter that is to be read. Moreover, opinions, criticisms, and questions by a student will seldom bless either the seeker or the speaker or the others in the meeting.

Remember that your meetings have a plan to be followed. Stick to it. There is no record that Bill Wilson cross examined Anne Smith before, during, or after she read from her Bible or from her journal. To the contrary, Bill said to T. Henry and Clarace Williams:

> I learned a great deal from you people, from the Smiths themselves, and from Henrietta [Seiberling]. I hadn't looked in the Bible up to this time, at all. You see, I had the experience [conversion experience at Towns Hospital] first and then this rushing around to help drunks and nothing happened (See Dick B. *The Akron Genesis of Alcoholics Anonymous*, p. 64).

Bill and Bob just listened to Anne's reading and comments, and learned. Discussions certainly were held between Bill and Bob for hours over many days, but not when a reading by Anne was in progress.

In your meetings, first comes the opening prayer, then the reading from James, then the reading from *The James Club and The Original A.A. Program's Absolute Essentials*, then the use of any suggested collateral literature, and finally audience participation.

Fourth, consider reading collateral literature

Devotionals: As you complete study of each Bible segment and my commentary on it, you might gain greater understanding or mental challenge by checking out the devotionals pioneers daily used to enhance their spiritual growth on that particular subject.

For example, you could go through *The Runner's Bible*, look for its comments on the James verses you have read. Then silently read those *Runner's* comments while the leader reads them aloud.

You may even wish to do the same thing with at least four other devotionals that were pioneer favorites: (1) *The Upper Room* by Nora Smith Holm. (2) *My Utmost for His Highest* by Oswald Chambers. (3) *Daily Strength for Daily Needs* by Mary W. Tileston. (4) *Victorious Living* by E. Stanley Jones.

All five devotionals were owned, used, recommended, and circulated by Dr. Bob. Several are mentioned in later A.A. "Conference Approved" publications.

Commentaries: There are several important commentaries on two of the three "essential" Bible segments that Dr. Bob read and recommended. These pertain to the Sermon on the Mount and 1 Corinthians 13. You can read Henry Drummond's *The Greatest Thing in the World* or Toyohiko's *Love: The Law of Life* for a commentary on Corinthians. It was studied a lot in early A.A. You can read any of several commentaries on the Sermon, all of which were read and used in early A.A.: Oswald Chambers' *Studies in the Sermon on the Mount*; Emmet Fox, *The Sermon on the Mount*; E. Stanley Jones, *The Christ of the Mount*. We haven't found any for the Book of James, other than verse by verse comments on certain James verses in *The Runner's Bible*, and also my own commentary in *When Early AAs Were Cured and Why*. There is also a further relevant collateral area you can pursue.

Shoemaker's titles: If you wish to see how many basic ideas from James influenced our founders and their mentors, you will find many specific references to James in the books written by Rev. Sam Shoemaker, Jr.

Other Literature: To sum up the collateral reading possibilities, you could use, and profit from reading, *DR.BOB and the Good Old-timers*; *RHS, The Co-Founders Biographical Sketches and Last Major Addresses*; Sam Shoemaker's *Realizing Religion*; and my titles *New Light on Alcoholism: God, Sam Shoemaker, and A.A.* and *The Oxford Group and Alcoholics Anonymous*

Fifth, open the meeting to relevant audience participation. Let individual students participate by presenting any desired discussion, comments, or questions about the James verses, or about the portions of my commentary they have just read, or about suggested collateral literature.

Audience participation does often have its place. It may help build mutual interest, friendships, and the feeling of belonging. It may, at the proper time, permit someone to let off steam. It may raise similar questions others have in mind. But it will probably be a rare moment if significant points are raised or answered. The leader should keep the participation short. Those who do present questions or comments should share with humility, patience, and tolerance. All should keep criticism, verbal reproofs, and lofty pronouncements to a minimum.

Three more suggestions: (1) Pray and ask for God's guidance before you speak—whether you are the leader or a member of the audience. (2) Keep difficult and extended questions for presentation or discussion until the meeting concludes. (3) You may even find it helpful to seek another source or religious authority for possible explanations.

As Bill Wilson wrote in his Big Book:

> There are many helpful books also. Suggestions about these may be obtained from one's priest, minister, or rabbi. Be quick to see where religious people are right. Make use of what they offer (*Alcoholics Anonymous*, 4th ed., p, 87)

AAs are seldom experts in either religion or medicine, and those present know it. Early AAs had good literature and good teachers to help and instruct them. They had Biblical books by the hundreds. They also had excellent teachers like Rev. Sam Shoemaker, Anne Smith, Henrietta Seiberling, and T. Henry Williams.

Today most groups would likely refuse admission to the likes of these proctors. And that is a sorry fact, though probably quite true. Suggest to people in your study meetings that they might want and need to invite outsiders to help in understanding the verses in James. But you had better place your shield in front of you, and expect an onslaught. The days when the likes of Father Ed Dowling and Rev. Sam Shoemaker were invited or even permitted to speak to AAs in meetings or conferences are, sad to say, all but at an end. It's hard enough to conduct a history conference without naïve objections and hindrances.

It's much harder to stimulate learning about the Bible and its relevance to the Big Book if you attempt to do so inside other A.A. meetings or groups.. Such an objective involves different and substantial challenges. There are wolves in the woods who don't like God, Jesus Christ, the Bible, religion, or church. They frequently turn a deaf ear to those subjects. Few members of this howling pack know anything about our history. Yet such bleeding deacons (though frequently outspoken, bold, and insulting) simply cannot and do not control or speak for A.A., its groups, or its meetings. But they try. In that vein, there are ongoing efforts today to remove the Lord's Prayer from meetings; to ban all kinds of literature—such as Fox's *The Sermon on the Mount*; to silence members who share about them; and to promote their views in A.A. conferences. Many times I've even heard obstructive remarks from those who oppose Big Book study conferences. And they are wrong!

Just gather a group of friends and interested parties in A.A. and then set up your own meeting—an A.A. meeting if that's what suits you. The James materials can be taught and learned. You are not in your meeting to lead, opine, or share, but rather to learn. Feel free to ask what you wish, state what you wish, and discuss what you wish. But when controversy arises, it is probably futile to promote your viewpoint in the meeting. In this respect, I'm reminded of the idea: "A man convinced against his will is of the same opinion still." Keep your controversial statements to yourself and present the point later to someone you think has the answers.

This discussion portion of a meeting follows the completion of reading from the Bible as well as the completion of reading from *The James Club and The Original A.A. Program's Absolutes Essentials*. Then it's open season.

Participants may have questions. They may have observations. They may have stories they want to share. And they may even be loaded with opinions. Hopefully they have already begun to see the relevance of James to Big Book or Twelve Step material. In fact, they can and should discover, from what has been read, the actual number of quotes and ideas from James that have still been printed and retained in the latest editions of A.A.'s Big Book. Participants should be encouraged to make observations about those facts. Such comments would be useful and would help underline what has been covered in the readings, Let all students raise questions, make observations, and give commentaries.

This portion of the meeting should be moderated by the leader, should proceed much as any A.A. discussion meeting proceeds. Audience comments should not be regarded as teaching or doctrine. Nasty, insulting, personal comments directed toward some individual should be reproved and silenced by the leader. Opinions can certainly be expressed. But definitive answers should be found through prayer, further reading of the Bible, further collateral literature, or from a knowledgeable priest, minister, or rabbi.

The more the questions the more the questioners may themselves see they what they still need to do, and profit from, their personal reading, independent of the meetings.

Close your meeting with the Lord's Prayer—just as the pioneers closed theirs.

Jesus' Sermon on the Mount

The Sermon on the Mount meeting or meetings should proceed in the same manner as the meeting or meetings on the Book of James. The same five approaches should be involved: (1) Pursuing the entire Sermon. (2) Reading every verse in it from Matthew 5 to 7. (3) Reading from *The James Club and The Original A.A. Program's Absolute Essentials*. (4) Reading suggested collateral literature. (5) Opening the meeting for discussion.

Bill W. and Dr. Bob each said many times that the Sermon on the Mount contained the underlying philosophy of Alcoholics Anonymous.

From what I have read in Alcoholics Anonymous literature, I suggest that Bill and Bob may have been referring to the entire Sermon, but more probably had in mind specifically the philosophy of the "Golden Rule" in Matthew 7:12: "Therefore, all things whatsoever ye would that men should do to you, do ye even so to them: for this is the law and the prophets." Possibly they may have thought of other verses as fundamental: (1) Matthew 6:10—"Thy kingdom come. Thy will be done in earth, as it is in heaven." (2) Matthew 7:21—"Not every one that saith unto me, Lord, Lord, shall enter into the kingdom of heaven: but he that doeth the will of my Father which is in heaven." (3) Matthew 5:43-44: Ye have heard that it hath been said, Thou shalt love thy neighbor, and hate thine enemy. But I say unto you, Love your enemies, bless them that curse you, do good to them that hate you, and pray for them which despitefully use you, and persecute you."

Taken together, the aforementioned verses emphasize ideas that have become pillars in A.A.—doing for others what you would like to have done for you; turning to God to see what He would have you do; loving your neighbor and even your enemies, and recognizing that God wants us to do His will as expressed primarily in His Word.

In your reading, you will soon discover a host of verses and ideas from the Sermon that became part of the fabric of A.A. For example, reconciling with your enemy; making restitution to those you have hurt; the Lord's Prayer; "first things first" as expressed in Matthew 6:25-33; "easy does it" as expressed in Matthew 6:24; inventorying and removing your own faults before you endeavor to have another's removed.

Begin the Sermon on the Mount meeting or meetings with prayer.

First, pursue all chapters and every verse in Matthew Chapters 5 through 7 inclusive. Follow our suggestions.

There is scarcely a verse in the Sermon that did not influence early A.A. actions, steps, and language. Thus, while James was the "favorite," the Sermon presented the greatest and broadest group of challenges. It spelled out most of the key aspects of a Christian way of life.

Second, study every verse in Matthew: 5, 6, and 7. The verses in those three chapters contain every word of the Sermon itself.

Following the same guide that was used as to James: Silently read, and have your leader read aloud every Chapter and every verse from the beginning of Matthew 5 to the end of Matthew 7.

Third, study the part of my title *The James Club and The Original A.A. Program's Absolute Essentials* that reviews and explains the verses in Matthew 5 to 7 you have just read. Compare each relevant segment of my title with the part or parts you have just read in the Sermon.

Fourth, consider reading collateral literature

Again the possibilities are similar to those discussed in conjunction with James.

Devotionals: You may choose to look into the five devotionals early AAs used and gain more understanding from the discussion of the verses you have read.

Commentaries: Unlike the situation with James, there are a host of writings on the Sermon on the Mount. In fact, it is often discussed in many of the books early AAs read for spiritual growth. But the following were studied extensively by Dr. Bob and some of the pioneers: (1) *Studies in the Sermon on the Mount* by Oswald Chambers. (2) *My Utmost for His Highest* by Glenn Clark. (3) *The Sermon on the Mount* by Emmet Fox. (4) *The Christ of the Mount* by E. Stanley Jones.

Other Relevant Titles: There certainly are other books that early AAs read and which contained references to, or studies of, various parts of the Sermon. You may want to locate them through two of my titles: (1) *Dr. Bob and His Library.* (2) *The Books Early AAs Read for Spiritual Growth*, 7th ed.

Fifth, open the meeting to relevant audience participation. Let individual students participate by presenting any desired discussion, comments, or questions about the Sermon verses, the portions of my commentary they have just read, or collateral literature they have considered.

Close the Sermon meetings with the Lord's Prayer just as the pioneers did.

The Thirteenth Chapter of 1 Corinthians

This widely read chapter in Corinthians has provided fodder for many a sermon on "love." There is scarcely an A.A. root source that doesn't make reference to this chapter. Its best known commentator was Professor Henry Drummond of Edinburgh University in Scotland. The professor delivered his address on Love in many places, including Africa; but its fame in America seemed to spring from his presentation in 1887 at a Northfield Conference. Drummond authored a number of popular books such as *Natural Law in the Spiritual World*, *The Ideal Life*, and the *Ascent of Man*. And when Dr. Bob's daughter Sue Smith Windows first opened her attic to the view of others, I discovered there that Dr. Bob had owned and read all the Drummond books. They were voluminous.

But the little book that caught my eye was a copy of Drummond's *The Greatest Thing in the World* (London and Glasgow: Collins Clear-Type Press, n.d.). Drummond fashioned the title from the last line of 1 Corinthians 13. Verse thirteen reads: "And now abideth faith, hope, charity [love], these three; but the greatest of these is charity." And various editions and reprints of this address have since sold in the hundreds of thousands. On page 26, Drummond wrote: "The Spectrum of love has nine ingredients:--Patience, Kindness, Generosity, Humility, Courtesy, Unselfishness, Good Temper, Guilelessness, and Sincerity." A moment's glance at the language of the verses themselves and then a glance at Drummond's characterization of them will call to your mind the principles of Alcoholics Anonymous.

Dorothy Snyder Murphy, the wife of pioneer Clarence Snyder at the time, often worked with drunks. On one occasion, she tells of this experience with Dr. Bob and Corinthians:

> Once when I was working on a woman in Cleveland, I called and asked him [Dr. Bob], "What do I do for somebody who is going into D.T.'s?" He told me to give her the medication, and he said, "When she comes out of it and she decides she wants to be a different woman, get her Drummond's "The Greatest Thing in the World." Tell her to read it through every day for 30 days, and she'll be a different woman" (*DR. BOB and the Good Oldtimers*, p. 310).

Now for your studies.

Open the Corinthians meeting with prayer.

First, pursue all chapters and every verse in 1 Corinthians 13. Follow our suggestions as to reading each verse and then comparing with my commentary.

Also as to reading collateral literature.

Finally, open the meeting to relevant audience participation. Let individual students participate by presenting any desired discussion, comments, or questions about the Corinthians verses, or about the portions of my commentary they have just read, or about the collateral literature.

Use the same five procedures for study of James, Matthew 5 to 7, and 1 Corinthians 13

■■■

Suggested Reading to Enrich Your Meetings and Individual Studies

As you complete study of each Bible segment, you might gain greater understanding or mental challenge by checking out the devotionals pioneers used. For example, you could go through *The Runner's Bible*, look for its comments on the subjects you have read, and silently read those portions as the leader reads them aloud. You can do the same with four other devotional favorites: (1) *The Upper Room* by *Nora Smith Holm*. (2) *My Utmost for His Highest* by Oswald Chambers. (3) *Daily Strength for Daily Needs* by Mary W. Tileston.(4) *Victorious Living* by E. Stanley Jones. And all four were owned, used, recommended, and circulated by Dr. Bob

There are several important commentaries on two of the three "essential" Bible segments Dr. Bob read and recommended. We haven't found any for the Book of James. But my latest title, *The James Club and The Original A.A. Program's Absolute Essentials*, will give you a heads up on the Book of James that will really help you.

There were several that explained Jesus' Sermon on the Mount: (1*)* *Studies in the Sermon on the Mount* by Oswald Chambers. (2) *I Will Lift Up Mine Eyes* by Glenn Clark. (3) *The Sermon on the Mount* by Emmet Fox. (4) *The Christ of the Mount* by E. Stanley Jones.

The all-out favorite discussion of 1 Corinthians 13 can be found in *The Greatest Thing in the World* by Henry Drummond. Glenn Clark also covered this "love" chapter in *The Soul's Sincere Desire*. Anne Smith quoted at length in her journal from Toyohiko Kagawa's Love: *The Law of Life*. Check Anne's comments and then Kagawa if you like.

It is no secret today that the greatest impact on Bill Wilson's Big Book and Twelve Steps came from the Oxford Group and from the teachings of its principal American lieutenant Rev. Sam Shoemaker. Word after word and page after page from Bill's writings came directly from the Oxford Group and Shoemaker, and Bill said so.

Our job here is to see how much the Oxford Group and Sam Shoemaker spoke about the Book of James, the Sermon on the Mount, and 1 Corinthians 13. I believe you will be best informed on these points if you read my two titles: *The Oxford Group and Alcoholics Anonymous* and *New Light on Alcoholism: God, Sam Shoemaker, and A.A.*

End

About the Author

Dick B. writes books on the spiritual roots of Alcoholics Anonymous. They show how the basic and highly successful biblical ideas used by early AAs can be valuable tools for success in today's A.A. His research can also help the religious and recovery communities work more effectively with alcoholics, addicts, and others involved in Twelve Step programs.

The author is an active, recovered member of A.A.; a retired attorney; and a Bible student. He has sponsored more than one hundred men in their recovery from alcoholism. Consistent with A.A.'s traditions of anonymity, he uses the pseudonym "Dick B."

He has had twenty-eight titles published including: *Dr. Bob and His Library*; *Anne Smith's Journal, 1933-1939*; *The Oxford Group & Alcoholics Anonymous*; *The Akron Genesis of Alcoholics Anonymous*; *The Books Early AAs Read for Spiritual Growth*; *New Light on Alcoholism: God, Sam Shoemaker, and A.A.*; *Courage to Change* (with Bill Pittman); *Cured: Proven Help for Alcoholics and Addicts*; *The Good Book and The Big Book: A.A.'s Roots in the Bible*; *That Amazing Grace: The Role of Clarence and Grace S. in Alcoholics Anonymous*; *Good Morning!: Quiet Time, Morning Watch, Meditation, and Early A.A.*; *Turning Point: A History of Early A.A.'s Spiritual Roots and Successes*, *Hope!: The Story of Geraldine D., Alina Lodge & Recovery; Utilizing Early A.A.'s Spiritual Roots for Recovery Today; The Golden Text of A.A.; By the Power of God; God and Alcoholism; Making Known the Biblical History of A.A.; Why Early A.A. Succeeded*; *Comments of Dick B. at The First Nationwide A.A. History Conference; Henrietta Seiberling: Ohio's Lady with a Cause;* and *The James Club*. The books have been the subject of newspaper articles and reviews in *Library Journal, Bookstore Journal, The Living Church, Faith at Work, Sober Times, Episcopal Life, Recovery News, Ohioana Quarterly, The PHOENIX,* and *The Saint Louis University Theology Digest.* They are listed in the biographies of major addiction center, religion, and religious history sites. He has published over 150 articles on his subject, most posted on the internet.

Dick is the father of two sons (Ken and Don) and has two granddaughters. As a young man, he did a stint as a newspaper reporter. He attended the University of California, Berkeley, where he received his A.A. degree with Honorable Mention, majored in economics, and was elected to Phi Beta Kappa in his Junior year. In the United States Army, he was an Information-Education Specialist. He received his A.B. and J.D. degrees from Stanford University, and was Case Editor of the Stanford Law Review. Dick became interested in Bible study in his childhood Sunday School and was much inspired by his mother's almost daily study of Scripture. He joined, and was president of, a Community Church affiliated with the United Church of Christ. By 1972, he was studying the origins of the Bible and began traveling abroad in pursuit of that subject. In 1979, he became much involved in a Biblical research, teaching, and fellowship ministry. In his community life, he was president of a merchants' council, Chamber of Commerce, church retirement center, and homeowners' association. He served on a public district board and has held offices in a service club.

In 1986, he was felled by alcoholism, gave up his law practice, and began recovery as a member of the Fellowship of Alcoholics Anonymous. In 1990, his interest in A.A.'s Biblical/Christian roots was sparked by his attendance at A.A.'s International Convention in Seattle. He has traveled widely; researched at archives, and at public and seminary libraries; interviewed scholars, historians, clergy, A.A. "old-timers" and survivors; and participated in programs and conferences on A.A.'s roots.

The author is the owner of Good Book Publishing Company and has several works in progress. Much of his research and writing is done in collaboration with his older son, Ken, an ordained minister, who holds B.A., B.Th., and M.A. degrees. Ken has been a lecturer in New Testament Greek at a Bible college and a lecturer in Fundamentals of Oral Communication at San Francisco State University. Ken is a computer specialist and director of marketing and research in Hawaii ethanol projects.

Dick is a member of the American Historical Association, Research Society on Alcoholism, Alcohol and Drugs History Society, Organization of American Historians, The Association for Medical Education and Research in Substance Abuse, Coalition of Prison Evangelists, Christian Association for Psychological Studies, and International Substance Abuse and Addictions Coalition. He is available for conferences, panels, seminars, and interviews.

Good Book Publishing Company Order Form

(Use this form to order Dick B.'s titles on early A.A.'s roots and successes)

Qty.	Titles by Dick B.	Price
_____	A New Way In	$19.95 ea. $ _____
_____	A New Way Out	$19.95 ea. $ _____
_____	Anne Smith's Journal, 1933-1939	$22.95 ea. $ _____
_____	By the Power of God: A Guide to Early A.A. Groups and Forming Similar Groups Today	$23.95 ea. $ _____
_____	Cured! Proven Help for Alcoholics and Addicts	$23.95 ea. $ _____
_____	Dr. Bob and His Library	$22.95 ea. $ _____
_____	Dr. Bob of Alcoholics Anonymous	$24.95 ea. $ _____
_____	God and Alcoholism	$21.95 ea. $ _____
_____	Good Morning! Quiet Time, Morning Watch, Meditation, and Early A.A.	$22.95 ea. $ _____
_____	Henrietta B. Seiberling	$20.95 ea. $ _____
_____	Introduction to the Sources and Founding of A.A.	$22.95 ea. $ _____
_____	Making Known the Biblical History and Roots of Alcoholics Anonymous	$24.95 ea. $ _____
_____	New Light on Alcoholism: God, Sam Shoemaker, and A.A.	$24.95 ea. $ _____
_____	Real Twelve Step Fellowship History	$23.95 ea. $ _____
_____	That Amazing Grace: The Role of Clarence and Grace S. in Alcoholics Anonymous	$22.95 ea. $ _____
_____	The Akron Genesis of Alcoholics Anonymous	$23.95 ea. $ _____
_____	The Books Early AAs Read for Spiritual Growth	$21.95 ea. $ _____
_____	The Conversion of Bill W.	$23.95 ea. $ _____
_____	The First Nationwide A.A. History Conference	$22.95 ea. $ _____
_____	The Golden Text of A.A.	$20.95 ea. $ _____
_____	The Good Book and the Big Book: A.A.'s Roots in the Bible	$23.95 ea. $ _____
_____	The Good Book-Big Book Guidebook	$22.95 ea. $ _____
_____	The James Club and the Original A.A. Program's Absolute Essentials	$23.95 ea. $ _____
_____	The Oxford Group and Alcoholics Anonymous	$23.95 ea. $ _____
_____	Turning Point: A History of Early A.A.'s Spiritual Roots and Successes	$29.95 ea. $ _____
_____	Twelve Steps for You	$21.95 ea. $ _____
_____	Utilizing Early A.A.'s Spiritual Roots for Recovery Today	$20.95 ea. $ _____
_____	When Early AAs Were Cured and Why	$23.95 ea. $ _____
_____	Why Early A.A. Succeeded	$23.95 ea. $ _____

(Order Form continued on the next page)

Good Book Publishing Company Order Form
(continued from the previous page)

Order Subtotal: $ _____

Shipping and Handling (S&H) **: $ _____

(** For Shipping and Handling, please add 10% of the Order Subtotal for U.S. orders or 15% of the Order Subtotal for international orders. The minimum U.S. S&H is $5.60. The minimum S&H for Canada and Mexico is US$ 9.95. The minimum S&H for other countries is US$ 11.95.)

Order Total: $ _____

Credit card: VISA   MasterCard   American Express   Discover   (circle one)

Account number: _____ Exp.: _____

Name: _____ (as it is on your credit card, if using one)

(Company: _____)

Address Line 1: _____

Address Line 2: _____

City: _____   State/Prov.: _____

Zip/Postal Code: _____   Country: _____

Signature: _____   Telephone: _____

Email: _____

No returns accepted. Please mail this Order Form, along with your check or money order (if sending one), to: Dick B., c/o Good Book Publishing Company, PO Box 837, Kihei, HI 96753-0837. Please make your check or money order (if sending one) payable to "Dick B." in U.S. dollars drawn on a U.S. bank. If you have any questions, please phone: 1-808-874-4876 or send an email message to: dickb@dickb.com. Dick B.'s web site: www.DickB.com.

If you would like to purchase Dick B.'s entire 29-volume reference set on early A.A.'s roots and successes (and how those successes may be replicated today) at a substantial discount, please send Dick B. an email message or give him a call.

Paradise Research Publications, Inc.
PO Box 837
Kihei, HI 96753-0837
(808) 874-4876
Email: dickb@dickb.com
URL: http://www.dickb.com/index.shtml
http://www.dickb-blog.com